BUSINESS COMPUTING PRIMER

BUSINESS COMPUTING PRIMER

Dr John S Edwards

Professor Colin D Lewis

Aston Business School

PITMAN PUBLISHING
128 Long Acre, London WC2E 9AN

A Division of Longman Group UK Limited

First Published in Great Britain 1994

© J.S. Edwards and C.D. Lewis 1994

A CIP catalogue record for this book can be obtained from the British Library.

ISBN 0 273 60005 2

Typeset by Vivitext Creative Services
Printed in England by Page Bros.

The Publisher's policy is to use paper manufactured from sustainable forests.

Contents

Preface

This book is intended to provide an introduction to the way in which computers are used in business. This necessarily entails giving a more general introduction to computing, but from a business perspective as opposed to a technological one. Our aim in writing the book is not to be 'driven by the technology', but to provide an introduction which concentrates on the ways in which business people use computers, and the management of computers in businesses.

Note that 'business computing' as we use the term here should be interpreted to include also the use of computers in the management and administration of public sector bodies and other non-profit organizations such as charities. Occasionally we will mention other, non-business, uses of computers as well, such as for games or mathematical calculations, principally to provide context or contrasts with the business-based material.

We have written this book primarily for first-year undergraduates on degree courses in business and management subjects, having lectured such a course at Aston University's Business School for many years. It should also be a suitable textbook for those doing joint degrees in business and other subjects (especially computer science), and for computer science students taking an option (or simply with an interest) in business computing. We hope it will also appeal to business men and women who have never formally studied computing, and also to A-level Business Studies students.

We have tried throughout to assume as little prior knowledge as possible of either computing or business, in order to produce a book accessible to anyone studying business computing. Readers with more knowledge may 'dip in and out' as appropriate; the structure of the book does not require that the sections be read in sequence from beginning to end. Our belief is that many new students of business will need to be told something about the tasks for which computer systems are supposed to be useful, as well as the systems themselves. We do not think it is sufficient merely to describe the technology and assume that the students can figure out how the technology applies to business.

Our intentions are therefore:
- to assume as little prior knowledge of computing or business as possible
- to concentrate on the business aspects of computing, i.e. those related to using and managing the technology and its development, not to building it
- to cover technical aspects only where business people typically get involved in technical aspects
- to give indications of where to go for further enlightenment

Our aim is not to turn business students into computing specialists (though perhaps some will be inspired in that direction!), but to enable them to get the best out of the computers they will use themselves, *and* to get the best out of the computer specialists who will be working with/for them.

Thus, for example, there will be little about programming in BASIC, because business users do not write programs in BASIC, except perhaps for some home computer hobbyists combining business with pleasure. However, it is worthy of some mention, as the programming language which readers are most likely to have heard of, and since it is necessary to know what programming languages in general are, and how they are used.

By contrast, the section on spreadsheets will go further into the 'nuts and bolts' of the topic, to discuss cell references and formulae, since a large number of business users do have to cope with these aspects on a daily basis.

Overall, we aim in this book to provide a sound basis on which the student can build, by further study and practical experience, to become both a capable business user of computers, and a capable manager of information technology in organizations.

John S. Edwards & Colin D. Lewis

Aston Business School, Birmingham, August 1993

Introduction

Computers are now used in almost every aspect of business life, and in almost every type of business. Large corporations rely on networks of computers to co-ordinate their activities. Indeed, many businesses, such as banks, would cease to function without their computer systems. Ask yourself a question: in what sense does your bank balance (whether you're in credit or overdrawn) really exist, except in the bank's computer records? At the other end of the scale, computers are now cheap enough to buy and the systems easy enough to use that many self-employed people do their own accounts on a personal computer at home.

It is fair to say that all business organizations in the UK of any reasonable size have at least one computer system. The proportion of those organizations employing 50 or more people which have one or more computers is so near to 100% that survey samples miss the very few without any. Even in the smallest of UK small businesses, those with between one and nine employees, the majority now have a computer, as the figures in Table 1 show.

Table 1 The take-up of computers by small businesses

(Survey by the UK Small Business Trust)

Number of employees	Proportion with a computer	
	1985	1991
under 5	25%	56%
5 – 9	29%	71%

The position is far from perfect, however. Many computer systems are not as easy to use as they ought to be, or do not do exactly what their users would like. Computing still has a mystique attached to it, and some people are, quite frankly, scared of computers. There are good reasons for this, some of which can be seen from a short history lesson.

The development of computers and other forms of IT (Information Technology) has usually been led by the scientific community, especially mathematicians (hence the name 'computer' — something that computes!). Business and management applications have tended to come rather later, and also to suffer from occasional handicaps due to the equipment's original purpose having been slightly different. It hasn't always been that way, and it doesn't have to be that way in the future (computer industry companies please note!).

Let's look back at an example from 'pre-historic IT', before the electronic age. You probably think of the abacus (see Figure 1), a frame consisting of a number of sticks or wires with beads sliding on them, as a children's toy. Actually it was designed as a piece of IT for commercial use — so that merchants and shopkeepers could work out how much their customers had to pay! Because it suits that purpose so well, it's still used in that manner in many parts of Asia and Eastern Europe.

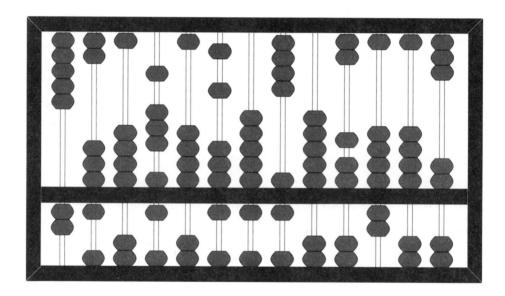

Figure 1 An abacus

Even punched cards (see Figure 2), those symbols of the computer revolution in the 1950s and 1960s, weren't originally associated with doing obscure calculations; they were originally devised by a Frenchman named Jacquard some 150 years earlier, in 1801, to control weaving looms so that they could produce cloth with a pattern. Even when they were first used for 'counting', it was with a practical purpose in mind when, in 1890, Herman Hollerith applied punched-card technology to the analysis of the US census results, reducing the time taken from years to months.

However, the first electronic computers *were* built for pure number-crunching, stimulated by World War II. Probably the first computer deserving of the name was Colossus, used by the Allied code-breakers at Bletchley Park. *Note that the argument over what was really the first computer continues to this day; in part, it depends on exactly what you mean by a computer. You don't have to worry about that here.* Machines designed for mathematical calculations such as ENIAC (USA) and EDSAC (UK) and the Manchester Mark 1 (UK) followed soon after the end of the war. Each of these three machines led on to commercial computers in the early 1950s: the Univac (made by Remington-Rand, now part of Unisys); the Lyons Electronic Office (LEO); and the Ferranti Mark 1 (Ferranti's computing division is now part of ICL), respectively. Most of the first commercial machines were originally bought by universities or research laboratories; it wasn't until 1953 or 1954 that serious business applications of computers appeared. This pattern of business computing applications being several years behind scientific and military uses has continued (with one exception which we'll mention shortly) ever since.

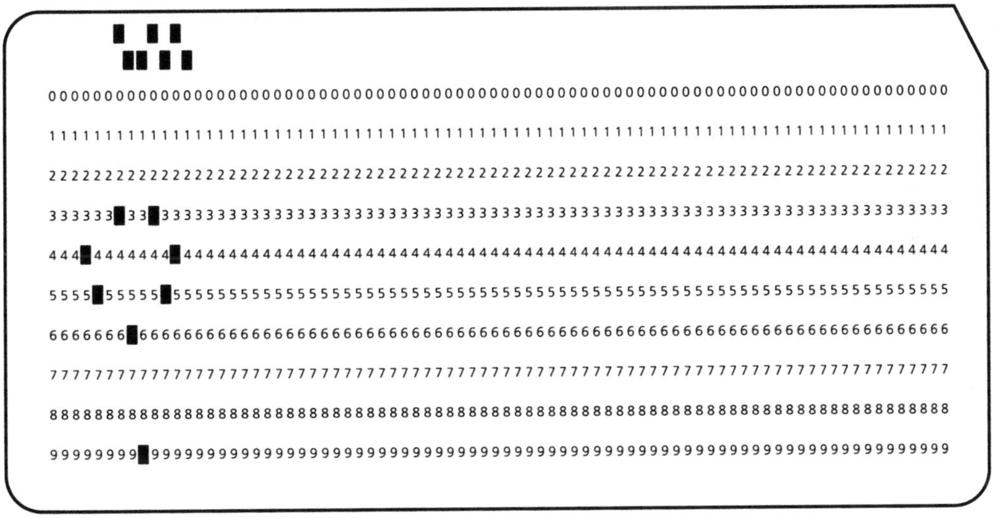

Figure 2 A punched card

In the UK, the first business computing application was the use of the LEO for payroll processing, i.e. working out how much each employee should be paid, how much tax to deduct and so on. It almost certainly pre-dated similar payroll applications in the US (but not by much!); exact dates are quite hard to come by for some of these developments, but for our purposes they are not important — the idea here is to give a general flavour of what happened. LEO had certainly been in use in tests since 1951. Lyons (now part of Allied Lyons) was not in the electronics business, but a food, grocery and catering company, best known for its chain of high street tea-shops which were a kind of 1950s equivalent of

McDonald's and similar fast-food chains today. The LEO computer was soon used for other work for Lyons, including processing the food orders from the tea-shops to give better despatch schedules (avoiding such things as making separate trips from the same warehouse to two neighbouring teashops on the same day), and giving management information on Lyons' tea stocks. One of the reasons for going into this level of detail here is that payroll, distribution scheduling and stock control are all typical business computing applications. Later the LEO took on outside jobs as well, including the payroll for the Ford Motor Company at Dagenham, calculating the Pay As You Earn income tax tables (which in pre-computer days helped employers work out how much tax to deduct each week) for the Chancellor of the Exchequer's budget, and some of the design work on the De Havilland Comet, the world's first jet airliner. Building on this pioneering work, Lyons did go into the computing business, selling 11 LEO IIs and 150 LEO IIIs, but the LEO disappeared in the 1960s, when Lyons' computing interests were taken over by English Electric, which itself later became part of ICL.

The three main advances as far as business computing is concerned (as we see them, at least) have come roughly 10 years apart since then:

- Widespread take-up of computers for batch applications such as payroll and accounts.
  Approximate date: late 1950s/early 1960s.
  Key events:
  (a) IBM 1401, first really large-selling machine (i.e. hundreds rather than tens), 1959.
  (b) J.Sainsbury, always among pioneer UK business users of computers and IT, bought its first computer in the same year.

- Introduction of interactive applications.
  Approximate date: early to mid-1970s.
  Key event: invention of the Visual Display Unit (in several places, more or less simultaneously), which made menus and form input possible.

- Advent of the PC (personal computer).
  Approximate date: early 1980s.
  Key events:
  (a) Visicalc, the first spreadsheet program, in 1979 (a business-led development at last!).
  (b) CP/M, the first disk-based operating system, in 1980.
  (c) IBM PC (USA 1982, Europe 1983), leading to ten-fold increase in micro-computer sales in one year.

On the basis of the 'ten year gap' rule, a fourth major advance seems to be due in the early 1990s; is it already happening? It's not easy to tell. The real significance of the first three advances only became clear with the benefit of hindsight. In the late 1980s, the leading candidates for the next advance appeared to be expert systems, also known as knowledge-based systems, and the electronic office (but remember what LEO stood for forty years earlier!). Both these developments, whilst useful, now seem to be falling some way short of revolutionary status. However, if tools to help groups of people work together, building on the networks which now connect formerly isolated PCs, fulfil their current promise, it may well be that the fourth major step forward is indeed in the process of happening!

Speculating about the future of business computing is, however, a dangerous activity. The UK business PC market was £285 million in 1982, and the *Financial Times* forecast in 1983 that it would be 'anywhere in the £2 billion to £4 billion range by the end of the decade'. In fact, the 1991 figure was £1672 million (i.e. £1.672 billion), and thus sales have not yet reached even the bottom of the predicted range. By business computing standards, this was actually a very accurate prediction! The error may well have arisen because the price of hardware per unit of processing power has decreased so much in recent years. More typical of the level of accuracy was the prediction made in the 1940s, before business computing had been considered, that the total world market for computers would be...about 20!

Fortunately for us, in the rest of the book we are concerned with the present (and sometimes, where necessary, the past) rather than with predicting the future. Table 2 summarizes the various elements of business IT which preceded today's business computers.

Table 2 Pre-electronic information technology in business/management

(Ac)counting	Abacus
	Mechanical calculator
Processing words	Typewriter
Controlling a process	Punched cards
Information processing	Punched cards (again!)

Before we go on: *Don't worry about any technical terms in this section which you do not understand. They will all be explained later in the book.*

Part A
BUSINESS COMPUTING ESSENTIALS

The key message in this section is that there are very few essentials in business computing. Really, there are only three fundamental things to understand:

- the difference between what the computer *is* and what it *does*

- the different rôles which people in organizations have with regard to business computing

- what the purpose of business computing is.

The first essential is to clarify two key words: you can't get very far in business computing without running into the terms *hardware* and *software*. The hardware is what 'the computer' is — what you can physically get hold of: the keyboard, the screen, the processor and so on (these terms will be explained in more detail in the hardware section of the book). The software ('the programs' — always spelt that way in computing circles, even in the UK) is what controls the hardware, and makes the computer *do* something useful. All computer systems have to have both hardware and software, because the hardware is no use without the software.

The difference between hardware and software. Think of a book (this one, even). It's printed on paper, and probably has a cover of thicker paper or cloth and board to protect the pages. The paper and the cover are the equivalent of computer hardware; the words and pictures are the software. Hardware without software is a book in which all the pages are blank.

In view of this, you may wonder why you need to worry about the distinction between hardware and software, or indeed why you have to worry about the hardware at all. (After all, you can read a book without worrying about how the pages are held together!) There are two basic reasons:

- the versatility of computer hardware

- the lack of standardization between different types of hardware.

Taking the first of these, the computer is a multi-purpose device, unlike a book, or even other electrical devices such as an electric kettle. The kettle only performs one function, heating liquid, so the only controls needed are to be able to start it and stop it; an on-off switch will do this well enough. Indeed, some kettles even switch themselves off when the water is boiling! The computer's processor (see section 11) isn't very different from an electric kettle or an electric light bulb, except that it has very many parts which can be switched on and off, instead of just one. So, in principle, the processor could be controlled by a series of on-off switches, and indeed that is exactly how the very first computers were 'programmed'. However, this method of giving instructions to the computer was both complicated and time-consuming. People in computing have therefore been working ever since the late 1940s on ways of making it easier to instruct the computer about what to do using a method that suits humans. What suits us best for giving instructions? A language. All software is basically a language for telling computer hardware what to do. This is covered in more detail in the software sections.

You may still feel that since the hardware is no use without the software, you only need to worry about the software. In an ideal world, this would be true; after all, you can drive a car quite happily without the slightest knowledge of how the engine or gears work. (Mind you, many people might argue that you could drive the car better if you do have some understanding of how it works.) This brings us to the second reason. Computing is still a relatively young and immature field compared to many engineering disciplines. Progress towards standardization is slow, and new hardware developments often mean that the capabilities of existing software have to be extended.

Computing isn't alone in this; it actually took a good many years for automotive engineers to come to any agreement on standardizing the major controls for cars. Using a steering wheel for directional control rather than a tiller or handlebars came quite early on; using pedals rather than, say, a hand throttle for controlling the speed came later; and having the pedals in the same order came later still; even now there is no universal agreement on where the handbrake is, let alone minor controls such as the ones for the lights and heating. Part of the reason for the time this process takes is that it is necessary to establish how people would like to control the car or computer, and then compromise between this and what is technologically possible.

At the present state of computer development, the limitations of the hardware still show through, and these are different for different types of computer system. That's why you do still need to know a bit about the hardware in order to use a computer system effectively.

Notice that if you do restrict the number of different tasks that a computer system is intended for, you can make it much more straightforward to use, and substantially reduce the need to worry about the hardware aspects. This has been most evident in the home in the success of computers intended for word-processing, such as the Amstrad PCW range in the UK, and for games, such as the products of Sega and Nintendo. Outside the home, perhaps the best examples are the ATMs (Automated Teller Machines) operated by banks and building societies.

We'll remind you again, though, that the hardware is no use without the software. We have to cover hardware briefly first for understanding — without it, some of the software section would not make sense to you — but for action, it's the software that counts. When thinking about a computer system to perform any task, it's always the capabilities of the software you should worry about first, even though the hardware manufacturers would like you to believe otherwise. After all, there's no point in buying a Ferrari if what you need a vehicle for is door-to-door milk deliveries! Note also that the times *are* changing. In the early years of computing, hardware companies tended to be much larger than software companies, whereas the reverse is now true. Indeed, most companies which began by selling hardware (even IBM) now derive a large proportion of their income from software.

The hardware and software problem applies at several levels, too. As well as the need for you to understand a bit about the hardware when you are sitting in front of a personal computer, the same problem applies to the organization as a whole. It is increasingly common for businesses to contract with an external company to be responsible not just for providing but also for running their computer hardware. This is known as *outsourcing* or *facilities management,* and perhaps the key example in setting this trend was when Eastman Kodak in the USA (the photographic company) contracted out all its IT provision to IBM. Again, if the hardware could be completely separated from the software part of the system, the user business could work on a hands-off basis, much as it might buy in its electrical power without being too worried about how that power is generated or supplied. However, the current state of development means that the user business still needs to have people who understand the limitations of the technology.

Let's turn our attention now to the second essential: who uses computers (and what they are used for). In the history part of the introduction, we identified some key business activities which computer systems help with. First, with routine administrative tasks such as calculations or filing. Next, interactive tasks, the most important of which is information retrieval. Next, support for the work of an individual manager. And now (but not finally), support for people working in groups.

It is important to realize that business computing means different things to different people, because of their roles. We identify four different types of rôle in Figure 3. Everyone plays the bottom one, that of computer user, and as we said in the introduction, this is for whom the book is written. Equally, just about every organization except the smallest has some staff in the next category, that of business system user/developer, i.e. the local computer wizard. However, the next category up will only exist in an organization that has its own business computing or information systems department; otherwise it will be filled by people from other organizations — services suppliers such as Andersen, Hoskyns, BIS and a host of others. The top category will not be in a user organization, but instead will be in hardware suppliers like IBM, ICL, DEC or Compaq; and software suppliers such as Lotus, WordPerfect and Microsoft.

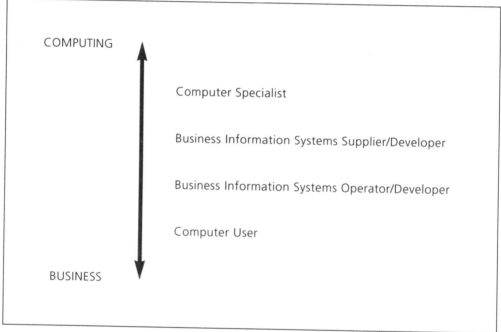

Figure 3 The different rôles in business computing

The third essential can be dealt with rather more rapidly than the other two: what is the purpose of business computing? Whatever some people may appear to believe, business computing for its own sake is a pointless activity. The sole purpose of business computing is to support and facilitate the activities of the business. The only organizations for which computing is an end in itself are those whose business is computing. There's a clear corollary to this: in order to work out what the computing needs of a business are, it is necessary to concentrate first on the activities which need to be supported or facilitated, rather than on the technological possibilities. This will be discussed further in Part D.

Finally, there is a fourth essential point to remember, concerned with 'hands-on' use of computer systems. While computer systems have many capabilities, they are totally stupid in one respect: everything you tell the computer will be interpreted literally. So, if you mis-type just one character when giving a computer an instruction, you will probably receive an 'error message'. Many people find this intimidating. Our advice to you is not to let it worry you. Treat the computer system as if it were a very young child that has to have everything explained in painstaking detail, or it will get it wrong. When an error appears the real fault is often not yours, but rather that the computer is far less able than humans to work out what you *meant,* as opposed to what you *said.* Researchers have made some progress in this direction over the years, especially in the area known as artificial intelligence, but most common business systems still take things absolutely literally. A more fruitful approach is to try to avoid typing things at all; the fewer things you type, the easier it is for you to avoid mis-typing them. Considerable developments have taken place in this respect in the last ten years or so, and some of them are described in the sections 1.1 – 1.4.

Part B
HARDWARE (1)

General description

The intention in this section is to give enough of an overview of hardware to provide a background for the software section of the book, as we mentioned in the Essentials section. A more detailed description of some aspects of hardware comes later.

Hardware is the term used in computing circles to describe the physical components that make up elements of a computer or a computer system.

Any computer system worthy of the name has to provide facilities for four tasks, namely input, processing, output and memory (or storage). Figure 4 shows a typical first-generation personal computer.

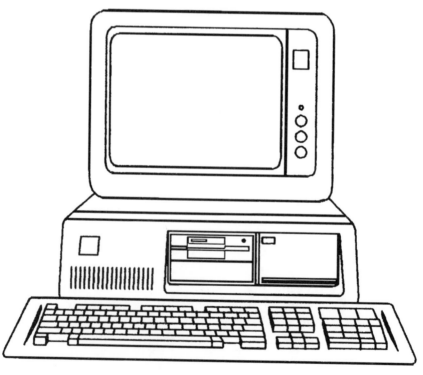

Figure 4 A typical first-generation personal computer

Input is telling the computer what to do.

Processing is the actual 'computing' — carrying out the instructions.

Output is reporting what happened; the results of the input and the processing.

Memory/storage is storing programs and data, both for use during the processing, and after the computer has been switched off, so that they can be retrieved and used again at some time in the future.

To clarify these terms, think of a basic model of a calculator; one with the four arithmetic functions and a single memory. It also performs these four functions, but in a more rudimentary way than computers do. You press a few buttons for the numbers and arithmetical symbols you want, maybe using the built-in memory keys, and up comes the answer on the display. Input is by you pressing the buttons. Processing is by the chip inside; that's why it's called a microprocessor. The processors in computers are similar but more complex. Output is a single row of digits, usually on a liquid crystal display. What's in the memory is usually lost when you switch the calculator off.

Input

The most common input devices are the keyboard (usually like that of a typewriter) and the point-and-click mouse, the latter being part of a so-called WIMP (Window-Icon-Mouse-Pulldown Menu) interface. These and others are described in more detail in section 10.

Processing

The overall 'label' of a computer is usually determined by its processor(s). The traditional description of processing hardware has been to divide computers into three types:

- mainframes
- mini-computers
- micro- or personal computers

This distinction is as much historical as anything; many of the mainframes still in use in businesses are less powerful than new 'top of the range' personal computers. Mainframes came first, the name coming from the big frames holding all the components together. Mini-computers were invented, and given their name, in the 1960s, era of the mini-car and mini-skirt; their big advantage over the mainframes was that they did not need a special environment, but could be put in any vacant office space. 'Micro' was the obvious name to choose for the next step down in size from a mini; a machine that could be put on a desk top. The boundaries between these categories are now extremely fuzzy, so we shall not be using these terms more than is absolutely necessary. Perhaps the key distinction is between a personal computer, intended for a single user, and all other types. Even this distinction is not clear, however. The term *workstation* is also often used. Originally, a workstation referred to a single-user system which would actually be powerful enough to support several users; effectively a mini-computer with only one user. Typically this was used for a special purpose requiring a great deal of processing power, such as computer-aided design. Nowadays, the term workstation is sometimes applied more loosely, to refer to any high-specification model of personal computer. We will try to use the term only in the former sense, where the distinction between workstations and personal computers continues to apply, even if expectations of what is the typical amount of 'power per user' continue to increase.

Still, at least all of the above three types of machine are relevant to most business uses, whereas the fourth category which has been added more recently, *super-computers,* is really only of use in scientific and military areas at present, where a great deal of out-and-out 'computing' is still required, such as for weather forecasting and for strategic defence work. The nearest that super-computers come to business use is in carrying out large-scale economic modelling, but this has not been particularly successful, for reasons to do with the validity of the models rather than the actual computing aspects.

What matters more than these labels is what you can *do* with the computers! (See the software sections.) A more technical discussion of processing issues appears in section 11.

Output

The most common output devices are the screen or Visual Display Unit (VDU), often called a CRT (Cathode Ray Tube) in North America, and the printer. The VDU is used for looking at the output now, and the printer for producing hard copy on paper so that you can look at it later, especially where no computer is available. These and others are described in more detail in section 12.

Memory/Storage

Computers operate with essentially two types of memory, usually termed internal memory and external memory. Internal memory is faster but volatile, i.e. when the computer is switched off such memory loses its stored information; in microcomputers it is usually electronic in nature, forming part of the processor chip. External memory is relatively slow but, accidents apart, permanent. Most commonly it takes the form of magnetic tapes or disks (the spelling with a k is becoming standard in computing). The phrase external memory arose because originally these were not permanently part of the computer, but had to be loaded specially as required; just as with music or video, where you have to find the tape or disk you need and put it into the player! The most common form of such external memory for a microcomputer is the floppy disk. However, nowadays some external memory is usually also located 'inside' the computer, in the form of one or more hard disks, so that you do not have to waste time searching for your programs and data files. As with recorded music, optical memory devices (CDs) are now beginning to challenge the magnetic ones as an external storage medium. Once again, these and other devices are described in more detail in section 13.

A note on bits and bytes, which form the basis of the units in which the size of computer memory is measured:

1 bit = 1 basic piece of information, i.e a 0 or a 1, corresponding to the two possible positions of an on-off switch mentioned in the Introduction section.

1 byte = 8 bits; this gives 256 different combinations of 0s and 1s (2 raised to the power of 8), which is enough to cover the basic set of characters used in computing, so 1 byte is effectively 1 character.

1 Kbyte = 1024 bytes or characters.

1 Megabyte = 1024 Kbytes or 1048576 bytes.

(These strange numbers are all powers of 2; the 'on-off switch' analogy again.)

We need to define two other commonly-used terms in this section; they are mainly found in connection with mini- and mainframe computers rather than personal computers. The first is a *terminal*. This is the standard input/output device through which a user interacts with a multi-user system; it consists of a keyboard and a VDU, and perhaps some other input devices as well, such as a mouse. However, it does not contain its own processor or memory/storage, so it is not a computer in its own right, although it looks very similar to one; it will not perform any useful function unless connected to a computer. We shall sometimes use the phrase 'terminal-based system' to refer to any multi-user system which does no local processing, i.e. as opposed to a personal computer-based system.

The second term is *peripheral*, more usually seen in the plural. The peripherals are all the parts of the computer except the processor(s): printers, terminals, tape drives, disk drives, etc.

Part C
SOFTWARE

Software is the set of instructions that makes the computer hardware do something useful (or indeed, anything at all!). We can look at this in two ways: from the user's point of view, and from the programmer's. For the user, what matters most is what software is available to help the business in its activities. There are three main categories of software: operating systems, programming languages, and applications packages, the latter ranging from the general to the specific; although as with all lists of categories, the boundaries between them are somewhat fuzzy. A brief description of each category follows: fuller details are given in succeeding sections.

Operating systems

An operating system consists of a series of programs which control a computer's internal organization and communications and as such must be loaded into the computer's internal memory before any applications packages can be run or 'high-level' (i.e. from the third generation or above; see section 2) programming languages used. Its function is rather like that of the rails on a railway; not much use in themselves, but essential if you want to run any trains (programs/packages).

Programming languages

These are the building blocks of which software application packages are made. Naturally these are the main concern from the programmer's point of view. Few business computer users or managers write their own programs, but a little appreciation of these software tools is necessary. In theory, any high-level programming language can be used with any operating system on any type of processor, by writing a *compiler* (a package which translates the programming language into the lowest-level instructions for the processor) for that combination, but in practice some combinations are much more common than others. Business users should be able to leave the computer specialists to worry about the details of compilers.

Applications packages

These are the major concern of the average business computer user. They range from very general applications which can be used right across a business, such as a database or graphics package; through applications for a specific function or type of task, such as personnel records, accounts packages or linear programming; to very specific applications such as an income tax calculation program or a sales order processing routine.

Table 3 Most common software packages (on personal computers)

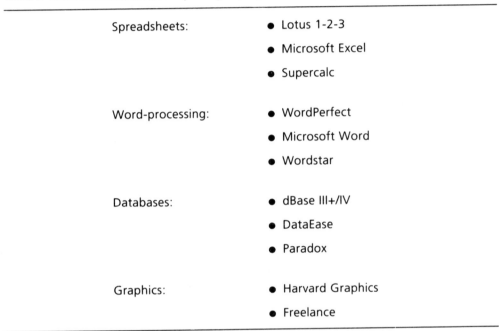

Spreadsheets:	● Lotus 1-2-3
	● Microsoft Excel
	● Supercalc
Word-processing:	● WordPerfect
	● Microsoft Word
	● Wordstar
Databases:	● dBase III+/IV
	● DataEase
	● Paradox
Graphics:	● Harvard Graphics
	● Freelance

What are the most common applications packages? The market tends to be looked at in different ways for the different sectors. On personal computers, the market statistics concentrate on sales of standard general-purpose packages. The most common ones in use are usually listed as spreadsheets, word-processing packages and databases, in that order, although there is a little uncertainty about the exact position as it is difficult to tell whether a new purchase is replacing an existing package or not. Table 3 shows the most common packages in the UK in 1992, and Table 4 shows the best-selling types of package in the UK in the year to March 1993. As may be seen, in terms of these current sales, where the figures are more accurate, word-processing packages and spreadsheets are still first and second, but now in that order, and accounts packages are now running ahead of database packages in third place. By volume, integrated packages, combining spreadsheet, word-processing, database and sometimes other facilities as well, are fifth. Presentation graphics packages have slipped back to sixth after a brief 'boom' period in 1991 when they were the latest thing in PC software. Language compilers, either for programmers to use, or for others to use the programs they have written, come next, and then computer-aided design packages. Note that the latter have a much larger market share by value because of their high unit price.

Table 4 PC software sales in the UK (year to March 1993)

	By volume	By value
Word-processing	25.4%	23.9%
Spreadsheet	20.3%	17.0%
Accounts	9.4%	12.6%
Database	6.8%	7.8%
Integrated	6.0%	3.5%
Presentation graphics	4.3%	4.1%
Language compiler	2.7%	0.9%
Computer-aided design	2.4%	7.5%

Source: *Computing*/Context.

On multi-user systems, the categorization of applications is usually by task or function, and the statistics are gathered by surveys of users rather than being based on sales by vendors. The most common applications (in alphabetical order) are:

● Accounting/billing

● Banking

● Manufacturing

● Order processing/stock control

● Payroll and personnel

● Purchasing

● Sales/distribution

Notice that even though banking applications are only relevant to a minority of organizations (banks and other financial institutions), they are so essential to these businesses that they still form a significant proportion of business computing applications as a whole.

The most common new applications (applications for which the organization did not previously use a computer system) being developed for multi-user systems, according to a survey carried out for *Computer Weekly,* were Executive Information Systems, Financial Control Systems and Decision Support Systems.

The succeeding sections look at various different types of software in more detail.

1 | Operating systems

In the sections on operating systems, we will devote most of the space to those which are found on personal computers, because those are the ones which cause the business user most immediate concern. You should not have to worry about operating system issues on a large, multi-user system, because there the operating system is taken as a 'given', at least for the user. On large systems, users may not even have access to commands at the operating system level. Such a situation would be very unusual with a desktop personal computer where, subject to company policy, a user could actually choose his or her own preferred operating system. Unless it is only to be used for a single application, then doing anything more than switching the computer on (even knowing when it may safely be switched off) generally requires some knowledge of the operating system.

One distinction worth making here is between the two basic modes of operation of a computer: *batch processing* and *interactive operation*. In batch processing, which was for many years the only mode possible, an entire series of operations is put together, and then executed by the computer without further intervention by the user. The failure of any one operation may mean the failure of the whole series, and thus final updating of data files usually takes place only at the end of the run. By contrast, interactive operation means that each command is obeyed immediately it is given, and the data files etc. are changed accordingly. A rough analogy is the difference between doing your own shopping (interactive) and giving somebody else a shopping list so that they can do it for you (batch). Having written out the list, it leaves you free to do something else, but it may not cope with unexpected events, such as choosing a substitute product for something which is out of stock.

The vast majority of business computing is now interactive, especially that done by managers, but there is still scope for batch processing in many organizations. Batch processing is particularly useful for financial transactions, where 'everything fails if one step fails' can be an effective device for security purposes. It is also a way of making more efficient use of the organization's IT resources, since batch processing can be done during the middle of the night when there are few, if any, interactive users. For these reasons, many bank ATM systems (see Part A) only update customers' accounts on a batch processing basis at the end of each working day, although some are truly interactive. *Try to work out which type your bank uses; one clue is that with a batch processing system you can only find out what your balance was at the close of business on the previous day, not what it is at this precise moment.*

The operating systems sections cover:

- DOS and other personal computer operating systems

- Graphical user interfaces (GUIs)

- Mainframe operating systems

- Unix.

1.1 DOS and other personal computer operating systems

In the first years of business microcomputing, prior to 1980, the programs comprising the operating system were recorded in ROM (Read Only Memory) chips and were, in effect, built into the computer as a permanent fixture. Later, in the early 1980s, when it became apparent that the expansion of the microcomputer market depended on communication between different manufacturers' machines via the exchange of disk files, disk-based operating systems became the vogue. The original disk-based operating system CP/M appeared with the early 8-bit microcomputers and their limited 64 Kbytes of memory, but with a common disk format. This allowed, for the first time, transfer of files between computers of different makes via floppy disks.

With the introduction to the UK of the 16-bit IBM PC in 1983, the operating system PC-DOS (Personal Computer – Disk Operating System), a joint development by Microsoft and IBM, became the standard operating system for 16-bit machines. Known as MS-DOS when applied to non-IBM machines, PC/MS-DOS became the industry standard, single-user microcomputer operating system.

The history of PC/MS-DOS, which was eventually to make Microsoft one of the most powerful players in the world-wide personal computer market, is fascinating. Bought by the founder of Microsoft, Bill Gates, for a mere $50,000 (then worth £21,500) from Satellite Computer Products as an operating system called 86-DOS, Gates and his associates re-wrote the package and licensed it to IBM as PC-DOS. Since every microcomputer sold requires an operating system, PC/MS-DOS was either sold separately or bundled with every IBM-compatible personal computer and, therefore, formed the basis of Microsoft's and Bill Gates fortunes, the latter estimated at $6.4bn or £3.4bn, making William H Gates III the richest man in the United States according to the 1992 edition of Forbes index.

When a microcomputer is switched on, its first requirement is to load the programs comprising the operating system. With disk-based operating systems such as DOS, this is achieved by saving the DOS system files within a special section of the first disk the computer attempts to read. Today, for the majority of microcomputers which are based on a hard disk configuration, given that no floppy disks are inadvertently present in additional floppy disk drives, the operating system files are loaded directly from the hard disk when the computer is switched on (i.e. the system is *booted*) and the computer is ready to operate, as shown by the familiar **C:\>** characters.

[For older microcomputers operating in a twin floppy disk drive environment, a system disk must be present in the default drive if the operating system is to be booted successfully and the dreaded **NON COMMAND DISK** message to be avoided.]

PC/MS-DOS

DOS (i.e. PC/MS-DOS) is effectively a command-driven package which is operated by a series of internal and external commands.

Internal DOS commands are always available when the main system file **COMMAND.COM** and associated hidden files are successfully loaded into memory. These commands cover the standard functions required of any operating system such as copying, erasing and renaming files, displaying directories, changing current date and time, etc.

External DOS commands are only available to the user when a file with a .COM extension of the same name is available on the disk. Thus the **FORMAT** command can only be executed if the DOS file **FORMAT.COM** is available. Other facilities available through the use of external DOS commands are disk copying, disk checking and support for graphics.

Originally the main function of DOS was indeed, from the user's point-of-view, a method of controlling disk operations. However, DOS is now required to perform many other tasks such as managing the configuration of the microcomputer's memory and configuring the various peripherals which might be connected, such as the keyboard, printer and to which port it is connected, the VDU, etc. To facilitate the initial configuration of a microcomputer's operating environment, the necessary DOS commands are usually stored in a special file named **AUTOEXEC.BAT,** and this file is loaded and executed automatically before the computer is available to the user.

Because DOS is required to cope with the needs of both the professional programmer and those of the average PC user, the complete operating system consists of some eighty commands, many of which have several options or alternatives. Although the average PC user only requires knowledge of five or six of these commands, to make life easier for users not prepared to learn the necessary syntax of the commands structure, a whole host of DOS interfaces have been developed by independent software houses which offer either:

- a menu-driven alternative (i.e. 1DirPlus, ProFinder, Pathfinder); or

- a WIMP (Windows, Icons, Mice and Pull-down menus) environment (i.e. Windows — discussed in detail in section 1.2).

As with most menu-driven or WIMP systems, DOS interfaces offer ease of operation to the novice but tend to obstruct the expert and mildly competent user. For instance, for the novice within a WIMP environment to point at an **ERASE** icon and subsequently point at a single file to be erased (or vice versa) followed by pressing a mouse button; or in a menu-driven environment, to *tag* a filename and then select the ERASE option within a menu; may appear much simpler than the equivalent typed DOS command which could be

ERASE WORDFILE.TXT

However, for the expert or mildly competent DOS user, knowledge of the DOS wildcard characters such as;

- * (representing any filename or any file extension) and

- ? (representing any single character)

allows for the use of concise DOS commands such as

ERASE *.*

which attempts to erase all files in the current directory but requires a confirmatory YES before doing so, or

DIR *.WK1

which produces a directory of only files with a .**WK1** extension, or

COPY CHAPTER? A:

which would copy the files **CHAPTER1, CHAPTER2, CHAPTER3,** etc. from the current directory to a disk in the **A:** drive.

More details of DOS commands are given in Appendix 1.

PC/MS-DOS has been the predominant microcomputer operating system during the 1980s and is likely to remain so for some time to come. To cope with the rapid development of microcomputers, new versions of DOS and equivalent systems such as Dr DOS are brought out by Microsoft and competitive software houses from time to time such that version 6.0 of DOS appeared in early 1993. However, as an essentially single-user microcomputer operating system, DOS has been condemned by the pundits in favour of the more powerful operating systems such as OS/2 and Unix. However, with Microsoft's massive investment in Windows to sit on top of DOS, in conjunction with most software developers' acceptance that the Windows environment is that which is likely to dominate the PC market over the next five years, the long predicted demise of DOS by the pundits seems as far off as ever. Rather like the four-cylinder internal combustion engine in the automotive market, which has also been derided since its inception as imperfect for its role compared with the *perfectly balanced* six-cylinder engine, DOS continues to flourish and will certainly be with us for some time to come.

Table 5 shows the market shares for operating systems on personal computers in Europe in 1992. Note however that the Windows share of the market is certainly increasing. As we write, in mid-1993, many personal computers are being shipped to customers with version 6.0 of DOS and version 3.2 of Windows already loaded onto their hard disks. This saves the users time in getting started, but also provides a bias towards using Windows or DOS rather than say OS/2 or Unix.

Table 5 Operating systems and market share

1992 market share of installed PC operating systems in Europe:	
DOS	76%
Macintosh	10%
Windows	7%
Unix	6%
OS/2	1%

Source: Ovum, *Software Product Markets Europe*

1.2 Graphical user interfaces

Until the mid-1980s, the basic operating systems and user interfaces of almost all computer systems were based around telling the computer what to do by typing in a series of instructions or commands. This style of operation is termed *command-driven,* for obvious reasons. It is also called *character-based,* because the computer interprets what you type one character at a time. Even though some systems had been developed which allowed the user to select what he or she wanted to do from a menu by typing just one letter (such as P for the command Print), or moving through choices using the Tab key, the whole system was still structured around typing in characters. The first real break away from this mode of operation, which goes all the way back to the days when the punched card was the main form of input, was developed in research work carried out by Xerox Laboratories in the USA. They developed the idea of the Graphical User Interface or GUI (pronounced 'gooey'). However, it was the

Apple Computer company which brought the GUI into commercial reality, with the trail-blazing Apple Lisa microcomputer, followed by the far more successful Apple Macintosh.

You may not realize that both Lisa and Macintosh are varieties of apple grown in the USA. Had the Macintosh been invented in Europe, it might have been called the Apple Golden Delicious.

The GUI is based around four components, often described by the acronym WIMP (which is NOT intended to be an insult!):

● Window

● Icon

● Mouse

● Pull-down menu

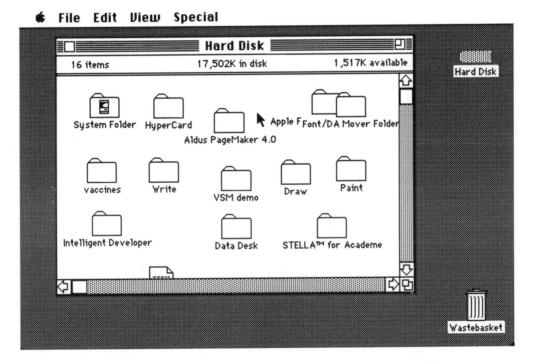

Figure 5 A graphical user interface screen (for the Apple Macintosh)

A typical GUI screen is shown in Figure 5 (for the Apple Macintosh). Window refers to the various rectangular boxes that appear on the VDU screen; the derivation of the name is obvious. You can change the size of the windows, move them around and so on. Icons are the little pictures used to represent programs and files, instead of just displaying a list of names, so that you can (if the icons are well-chosen) distinguish between different types of file or program at a glance. The mouse (see section 10.2) is used to move a pointer on the screen. This is the crucial difference between a graphical interface and a character-based one; the basic action is point and click, rather than pressing a key. Originally the P in WIMP stood for Pointer, but somewhere along the line it was changed, probably because it was realized that the term Mouse covers the same component, and that something was being left out. That something turned out to be the Pull-down menus; pointing at one of them gives a menu of commands from which you can select, again by pointing.

GUIs were also introduced for the specialized workstations used in Computer-Aided Design and Artificial Intelligence (see sections 3.19 and 3.16), and their evident success prompted a race to develop a GUI for the IBM PC-compatible hardware platform. IBM themselves came to the starting line first, with their OS/2 operating system with its Presentation Manager GUI. OS/2 is still around, and has a noticeable market share, but the winner at present appears to be Microsoft with its Windows operating system. Opinion about Windows seems to be divided between those who come to it from a DOS background, who generally see it as a great improvement, and those who come from an Apple Macintosh background, many of whom regard it as a slightly inferior attempt to offer similar facilities. Figure 6 shows a Windows screen; compare it with Figure 5.

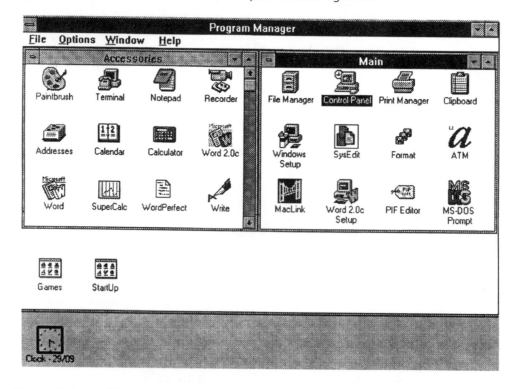

Figure 6 A graphical user interface screen from a Windows environment

Pursuing this point further, there are two reasons why many people feel that the Macintosh GUI still has the edge over the various GUIs for IBM-compatible machines. One is the existence of the so-called 'common user guidelines' which ensure a very high degree of similarity between different applications packages on the Macintosh. Experienced Macintosh users can normally start using a new Macintosh package without looking at the manual. The other reason is that the Macintosh GUI actually *is* the Macintosh operating system, whereas Windows still has DOS 'underneath' it. DOS 'shows through' the functionality of Windows in the same way that the computer hardware sometimes shows through the software, as we have mentioned already.

In addition to these operating systems specifically designed for them, personal computers are now powerful enough to run operating systems originally designed for larger machines, most importantly the Unix operating system (see section 1.4). Unix, although not a GUI itself, now has several competing GUIs associated with it, versions available to run on personal computers including X-Windows, Unixware, Open Desktop, NextStep and Solaris. With improvements to existing operating systems, new developments such as Windows NT, and (no doubt) entirely new systems, the operating systems battle is certainly not over yet!

A cautionary tale. The original Apple Lisa was not a tremendous commercial success, although it created a great deal of interest. This was because it moved so far away from a character-based interface. Except for operations which could not realistically be done without using the keyboard, such as typing in a word or a number, everything **had** *to be done by using the mouse to point at the relevant icon or menu item on the screen. This proved to be excellent for new users, but soon became annoying for more experienced users, since there were no short-cuts available for frequently-used commands such as 'Save' or 'Print' or 'Help'. To its credit, Apple Computer was alert to these criticisms, and was sufficiently far ahead of its competition that it could still produce the improved GUI operating system of the Macintosh well ahead of the opposition.*

1.3 Mainframe operating systems

Everything that we have already said about operating systems on personal computers applies equally well to mainframe systems, but there is also an extra level of complexity. This arises because a typical personal computer has one user, one VDU screen, one printer, one hard disk drive and so on, whereas the typical mainframe has many users (probably all performing different tasks), many storage devices, many output devices and so on.

Thus a major issue with mainframe operating systems ever since computers first became multi-tasking systems has been how to manage the allocation of the computer's resources between the tasks and ensure that different tasks do not interfere with each other. Note that, strictly speaking, a computer with a single processor cannot actually perform more than one task at a time; what it actually does is to devote a small amount of time to each task in turn, rather like a chess Grand Master playing 25 opponents simultaneously. It does it so quickly that the delay to one task caused by the time spent on the others is not apparent.

When interactive computing arrived, the multiple tasks became multiple users as well. The problem then arose of making sure that each user only accessed the parts of the system which they were permitted to, irrespective of the other tasks which the computer was doing at the time. This was (and is) usually done by a system of user identifiers and passwords (see section 9).

Well-known operating systems such as VME or VM or MVS on IBM mainframes, or VMS on DEC mini-computers, often show their 'punched-card' ancestry, as does even DOS on PCs. One example of this, which applies to DOS and VMS amongst others, is that if you want to see the contents of a file on the VDU screen, the command you type is 'Type'. This effectively indicates a mind-set that goes back to the days before VDUs were in use, when interaction took place via a machine called a teletype, which looked rather like a typewriter. 'List' is only marginally better for this command. Some of the more modern operating systems at least use 'View', while most of the GUIs do not distinguish between looking at the contents of a file and working with them — the command 'Open' in both Macintosh and Windows environments allows you to both see the contents and work with them, and of course a GUI user can simply do this by pointing to the appropriate Icon and clicking the Mouse button twice anyway!

1.4 Unix

Originally, operating systems were associated with a particular type of hardware; at one extreme this might be just one machine range from one supplier, or at the other, all machines based on a particular kind of processor chip. Unix was created as an attempt to avoid the limitations which result from this convention, and to be usable across a wide range of different machines from different hardware manufacturers with widely different internal *architectures*, i.e. different processor chips, communication systems, etc.

As such, it has become associated with the Open Systems movement, which consists of people who would like to see a system whereby computer hardware from any two manufacturers could be straightforwardly connected together. Unix is also closely linked with the language C (see section 2.4), for which similar advantages are claimed.

Unix succeeded initially in the workstation market rather than in the data processing or personal computing markets. This was partly because of a reputation it acquired for being more difficult even for the computer specialists to deal with; a natural difficulty arising from the need to cope with different hardware which prevented the use of 'short-cuts'. Not surprisingly, this meant that computer specialists with knowledge of Unix commanded higher rates of pay than other specialists. This additional expense was more easily justified in supporting the typical professional user of a special-purpose workstation such as an engineer or architect, the basic cost per user of providing workstation facilities being much higher than for data processing or personal computing anyway.

Supply and demand mean that the cost differential has decreased as the use of Unix has become more widespread, especially in educational institutions (see Table 5 in section 1.1), but its reputation for greater difficulty still remains. Its major strength is that, unlike all the operating systems which preceded it (and most which have been developed more recently), it can be used on any type of hardware, ranging from personal computers to super-computers. Most other operating systems have been tied to a particular type of computer, such as DOS to IBM-compatible personal computers, Digital's VMS mainly to mini-computers, and IBM's VM and VME to mainframe computers.

For an example of the flexibility of Unix, the venture capital company 3i, based in Solihull, uses the Unix operating system for all its computer systems. This involves some 250 personal computers of various makes, plus 400 terminals used to access larger computers (32 Unisys machines and 12 Hewlett-Packard); the personal computers can also access the larger machines. Reliance on Unix considerably reduces problems of communications and interoperability.

2 | Programming languages

Programming languages are the means by which the computer software is actually put together; the language in which the instructions are given to the computer hardware. Anything you want the computer to do will mean either writing programs (to remind you again, the American spelling of program is the one used in the computer world) yourself, or using a program which someone else has already written.

The aim of a programming language is to translate what you want to do from terms which you can understand into terms which a computer can understand. Since all a computer can 'understand' in any meaningful sense are the terms 'on' and 'off', a lot of translating needs to be done. In fact, the first computers were literally programmed by physically moving hundreds of switches into the right positions. It's become a little easier than that now, but not all that much.

In general, programming languages have shown two distinct tendencies over the past 40 years. The first is a gradual move away from instructing the computer in precisely *how* to do things towards 'merely' telling it *what* to do. The second is a move away from instructions in a form which suits the computer (i.e. numbers) and towards instructions which look more like the natural languages which we use to communicate with other people — at least, those languages of the English/French/German type (but not Chinese or Japanese). These two tendencies usually go together, but not always, as we'll see in a moment. *{Note that most new programming languages are usually described in their advertising as being 'English-like'; this has been the case for at least 30 years!}*

Programming languages are currently often divided into five generations, and this is not just for historical reasons, especially from the programmer's viewpoint, because all five of the generations remain in use.

In first-generation languages, the instructions are given in what is called machine code. Each operation has its code number, and just to make it even harder for the humans, these numbers are typically not based on counting in tens the way we do, but on counting in twos (binary), or sixteens (hexadecimal). Perhaps you can see the resemblance between counting in twos (where the only digits are 0 and 1), and the on-off switches mentioned above; if 0 means 'off' and 1 means 'on', then a binary number corresponds precisely to the setting of a series of switches. This is no coincidence; again the idea is that everything is designed to suit the machine. Generally speaking, programs written in machine code are meaningless except for that particular type of machine.

Second-generation languages, usually known as assembly languages or Assembler, replaced the arbitrary labels for operations of machine code with sets of instructions which at least meant something, like using A for Add and so on. However, there were still usually different sets of instructions for each type of machine.

Third-generation languages, although dating from the 1950s, still form the majority of programs in use today, and are therefore what people mean when they refer to 'conventional programming languages'. In third-generation languages, commands are English words like PRINT. These languages were specifically designed so that they could be used on different types and different makes of computer, although a certain amount of minor translation is still required, in much the same way that American English is not exactly the same as 'English' English.

Fourth-generation languages or 4GLs were given that name as a deliberate marketing ploy, to show that they represent an advance on third-generation languages. A typical statement in a 4GL looks more like English (rather than the semi-mathematical appearance of, say, FORTRAN). There is also no need to specify every single step in the series of instructions.

Up to this point, there is general agreement on the classification, and progress is clear on both counts mentioned above (towards a language that suits the human user rather than the computer, and towards the 'what' instead of the 'how'). There is, however, less agreement on the so-called fifth-generation languages. These languages, generally associated with work on artificial intelligence, were given the name 'fifth-generation' because one of them, Prolog, was chosen as the main language in the Japanese Government's Fifth Generation Computer project.

There is no doubt that these languages progress even further towards concentrating solely on 'what' is to be done than 4GLs do. Indeed, in many cases the precise order of the statements in a program written in a fifth-generation language is irrelevant. However, they do not appear to pass the test on the 'more like human language' criterion; fifth-generation languages such as Prolog and LISP (see below) are no more like natural language than typical third-generation languages. Table 6 summarizes the characteristics of the five generations of programming languages.

Table 6 The five generations of programming languages

First generation	Machine code (binary, hexadecimal, etc.). Instructions meaningless except for this particular type of machine.
Second generation	Assembler — instructions which mean something, like A for Add and so on
Third generation	Conventional (declarative) programming languages (as above). Commands are now words like PRINT.
Fourth generation	4GLs. Syntax looks more like English (rather than mathematics). No need to specify every step.
'Fifth generation'	Declarative or non-procedural languages. Prolog and LISP — no need even to say what is to be done!

Example of language generations (based on instructing a person, rather than a machine):

It is the end of a gruelling Business Computing lecture (gruelling for the lecturer, that is...). Our lecturer is in danger of collapse from hunger. He gasps to a student. 'Here's some money. Go over to the common room and buy me a Mars bar, please.' Let's take this as a rough analogy with a statement in a good 4GL. Note that some things haven't needed to be said, such as where the common room is, or '...and bring it back here', which is presumably implied by 'buy *me* a Mars bar' rather than just 'buy a Mars bar', which might imply the student should eat it, too. It might be a good idea to be specific about what happens to the change, though!

To achieve the same in a third-generation language, the instructions would have to be at the level of: 'get up, go to the door, go out of the door and turn right...' — and crucially the lecturer would have to tell the student all about bringing it back again, in the same level of detail. At second-generation language level, the lecturer would be saying: 'straighten your legs, push up with your arms, turn to your right through 90°...'. At machine code level, the lecturer would have to send out the signals from the brain to the nervous system that make the student do all those actions, i.e. moving to a non-verbal level.

What about a 5GL? Ideally, the lecturer would give the money to the student and smile, and the student *knows* he always wants a Mars bar at the end of a Business Computing lecture! The best of current practice is probably equivalent to saying 'Mars bar?', or just possibly 'I'm hungry'.

Take heart from the fact that few managers ever need to write a program in a programming language as part of their work. However, it is worth saying a little more about some of the ones you are most likely to encounter. As a manager, you will certainly be responsible at some stage in your career for buying or commissioning some programming work, possibly from expensive consultants. Perhaps the most well-known programming languages are FORTRAN, COBOL and BASIC, although there are many others such as PASCAL, APL, Prolog, LISP and C. Table 7 shows the most commonly-used programming languages. The divisions in the programming language 'market' are perhaps not quite as simple as a tongue-in-cheek mid-1980s description suggested: 'a lot of scientists programming in FORTRAN, a lot of schoolchildren programming in BASIC, and a lot of business people using programs in COBOL'. Nevertheless, this does give some idea of the state of affairs. Here we briefly describe FORTRAN, COBOL, BASIC, C, Prolog and LISP.

Table 7 Most common programming languages used

On micros	BASIC	
	C	
On minis	COBOL	28%
	RPG	23%
	BASIC	12%
	FORTRAN	12%
On mainframes	COBOL	70% +
	Assembler	12% (!)
	PL/I	7%

2.1 FORTRAN

FORTRAN, which stands for FORmula TRANslation, was developed in the 1950s primarily for the scientific computing applications which then dominated computer use. It was designed to make it easy to represent the mathematical equations typical of scientific calculations, and it had the backing of IBM, already a powerful computer company even then.

Several improved versions of FORTRAN have appeared over the years, such as FORTRAN4 and FORTRAN90 (no, there weren't 85 others between those two). It still has a central place in scientific and mathematical computing because of its standardization and its links with IBM, though it has always had some weaknesses from the business applications point of view. For example, printing facilities were somewhat weak for many years; the expectation of those who designed FORTRAN appeared to be that output as well as input would be on punched cards.

2.2 COBOL

Given FORTRAN's scientific bias, it is not surprising that as business uses of computers increased, there was soon an attempt to produce a programming language more specifically suited to business applications. One of the key differences between the two types is that scientific applications typically involve relatively little data input, but very sophisticated calculations, whereas business applications typically perform relatively simple calculations on very large amounts of data.

The surprise about COBOL (COmmon Business-Oriented Language) was therefore not that it was invented, but that it was commissioned by the U.S. Department of Defense! This is not as odd as it may seem, because running a large military organization gives rise to considerable problems of management and administration connected with payroll, accounts, personnel, supplies and so on. COBOL is structured around activities such as processing data and producing reports, and as business computing has overtaken scientific computing, so it has become the most commonly-used programming language in the world. This is particularly true of the very largest systems, such as those used by banks, insurance companies, government departments and major industrial and commercial firms. It has been estimated that more than 60% of all the programs currently in use are written in COBOL.

2.3 BASIC

If you've encountered a programming language in school, it's most likely to have been BASIC. Originally developed in 1964 by Kemeny & Kurtz of Dartmouth College, USA, the name is an acronym for Beginners' All-purpose Symbolic Instruction Code; it was designed to help teach programming to beginners. Where it really took off, however, was with the microcomputer boom of the late 1970s. Almost every microcomputer came with BASIC either available for it, or indeed built-in, as happened with the IBM PC microcomputers. BASIC thus became the staple language of the home computer software market, whether for games or for doing the accounts for a household or small business.

2.4 C

C is somewhat newer than the other languages mentioned here, and is growing rapidly in popularity. It was originally closely linked with the Unix operating system (see section 1.4), having been invented by the Bell Telephone Laboratories in the USA specifically to write the programs which make up Unix. Partly as a result of that, C has been designed to be very *portable*, i.e. programs in C are able to be used across a wide range of different hardware and operating systems with relatively few modifications. (*You might say that there were fewer differences between the different 'dialects' of C.*) It has therefore succeeded in taking a proportion of both the BASIC and FORTRAN sectors of the market, and even a little of the COBOL territory as well. It is probably the most popular language for writing packaged software at present.

2.5 Prolog and LISP

These two languages are the most well-known of the declarative or 5th-generation languages. Both were originally developed for work on artificial intelligence — LISP as long ago as the 1950s. LISP stands for LISt Processing, Prolog for PROgramming in LOGic; and, as may be inferred from these names, both were designed for very different tasks from FORTRAN. During the artificial intelligence (AI) 'boom' of the 1980s, LISP and Prolog were very much the two opposing contenders to become the leading language for AI work, LISP being the American candidate and Prolog the European one. Prolog was not taken very seriously in the USA until it was adopted by the Japanese as the language for their Fifth Generation Computer Project in 1982. Now that the AI hysteria has died down, it is seen that both languages have their strengths and weaknesses for AI work, and that both have the potential to be used in some areas outside AI.

3 | Application packages

The vast majority of the work which managers do on a computer consists of using applications packages written by others. As we have said before, very few managers write programs or applications packages for themselves. Such applications range from extremely general ones such as electronic mail, where the facilities needed are very much the same irrespective of the organization and an individual manager's rôle within it, to those which have been specifically developed to meet the needs of a certain group of users within a particular organization, such as the software which maintains the records for the Universities and Colleges Admissions Scheme (UCAS) through which most UK students' applications for first degree courses are processed. These two extremes are the equivalent of buying clothes 'off the peg' or 'made to measure' respectively, and have roughly the same virtues; 'off the peg' is quicker and cheaper, but 'made to measure' ought to fit better. There's an intermediate position too; that of customizing a general package to suit your needs better (like buying a pair of trousers 'off the peg' and then having the legs shortened). This is becoming more common because of the relatively low price of software packages. These issues are discussed at greater length in Part D.

In the sections which follow this one, we will describe both general applications packages and more specific examples. For obvious reasons we will devote the most space to those which are most general (and therefore also most common) such as spreadsheets and databases, although the more technical material relating to these two is separated into Appendices.

3.1 Spreadsheets (1)

Basic concept

Of all the applications packages which have become widely available since the development of the personal microcomputer, spreadsheets have had the greatest impact in promoting the use of microcomputers amongst non-specialist computer users. While word-processing and flexible database packages have mainly been developed from parent mainframe equivalents, the development of spreadsheet packages has been linked almost totally with microcomputers. This occurred to such an extent that in the early days it was often claimed that a high proportion of microcomputers were sold simply because their potential users wished to run a spreadsheet package.

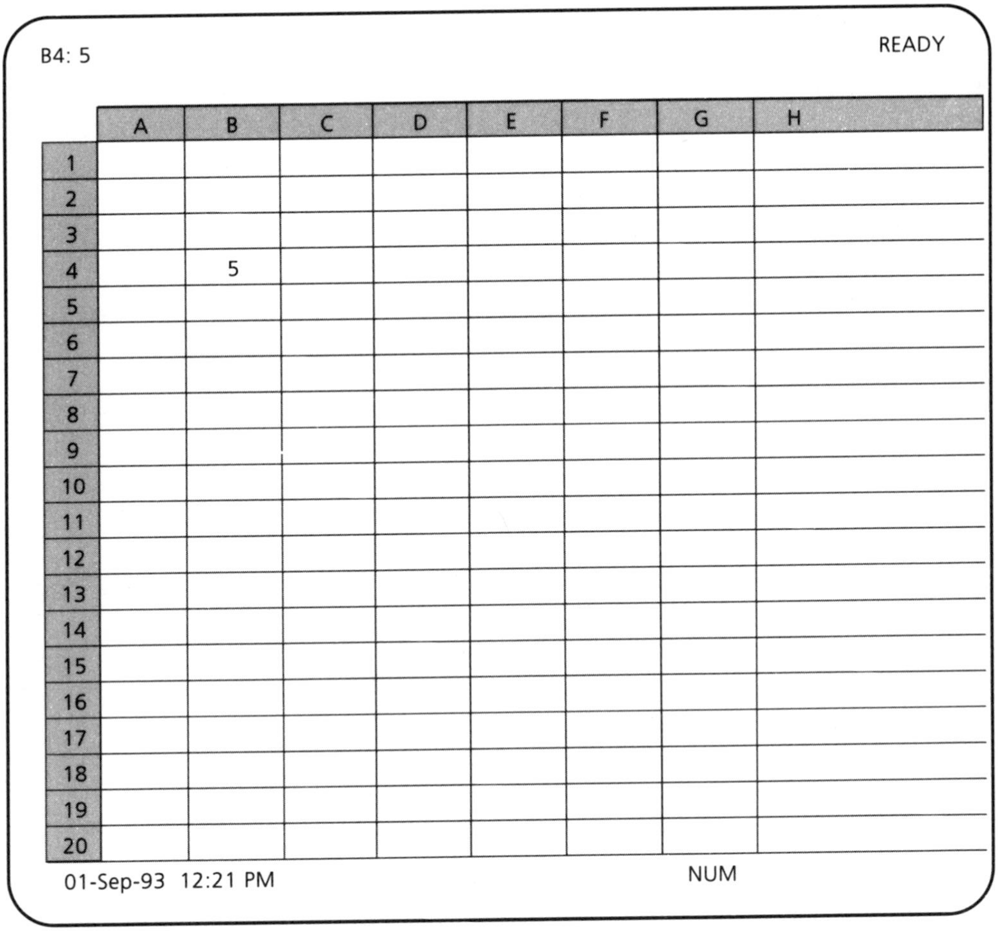

	A	B	C	D	E	F	G	H
1								
2								
3								
4		5						
5								
6								
7								
8								
9								
10								
11								
12								
13								
14								
15								
16								
17								
18								
19								
20								

01-Sep-93 12:21 PM   NUM

Figure 7 An example of a spreadsheet

The spreadsheet package was designed to look like the (paper) worksheets used by accountants, i.e. a grid of rows and columns. An example screen in shown in Figure 7. The computer-based version relies on the simple concept, originally conceived by a Harvard Business School student Daniel Bricklin, that within a two-dimensional array with lettered columns and numbered rows, a mathematical variable is defined completely by the letter and number corresponding to its position within the two-dimensional array. Hence for example, simply entering the number 5 at the intercept of column B and row 4 (i.e. at the cell referred to as **B4**) effectively defines a variable named **B4** as being equal to 5. Subsequently, any equation within the spreadsheet which refers to **B4** will assume that value of 5 or, more interestingly, the current value held at **B4** — which although originally set at 5 can be changed at any time. This is the great advantage of the spreadsheet over its paper predecessor; any changes to one value may be automatically reflected in all the other values (totals, sub-totals, ratios, percentages) which depend on that one.

This facility allows users to investigate alternative solutions to relatively complex problems, with the associated arithmetic being performed automatically by the spreadsheet package. It was such an advance on both paper systems and earlier computer software that it was often referred to as a 'what if' facility, because it answers questions such as 'what happens if we do this...?'. As an example of this facility, examine the BREAKEVEN ANALYSIS shown as Figure 8. Here clearly the profit or loss made by selling **E8** units will be equal to the net profit per unit (PRICE − TOTAL VARIABLE COSTS or, in spreadsheet terms, **C3 − C19**) multiplied by the number of UNITS SOLD **E8,** minus the TOTAL FIXED COSTS **C10,** i.e.

+E8*(C3 − C19) − C10

	A	B	C	D	E	F	G	H	I
1			PROFESSOR LEWIS'S SUMMERTIME CATERING COMPANY						
2			-------------	--------	---------	-------	----	--------	--
3	PRICE...		6. 00		BREAKEVEN.......	.5			
4									
5					MEALS	PROFIT			
6	FIXED COSTS				SOLD	OR LOSS			
7	RENT		4. 00		----------	--------	------	----------	
8	TRANSPORT		12. 00		1	-12. 70			
9			-------------		2	-9. 40			
10			16. 00		3	-6. 10		MEAL RANGE	
11			-------------		4	-2. 80		SETTINGS	
12					5	0. 50		=======	
13					6	3. 80		START. ...1	
14	VARIABLE COSTS				7	7. 10		INTERVAL .1	
15	FOOD		2. 00		8	10. 40			
16	LABOUR		0. 50		9	13. 70			
17	O'HEADS		0. 20		10	17. 00			
18			-------------		11	20. 30			
19			2. 70		12	23. 60			
20			-------------		13	26. 90			

Figure 8 A spreadsheet showing a breakeven analysis

Any change in any of the values of:

- UNITS SOLD (**E8** to **E20**) which are themselves dependent on the START value and INTERVAL value

- PRICE **C3**

- TOTAL VARIABLE COST **C19**, itself dependent on costs of FOOD **C15**, LABOUR **C16** and O'HEADS **C17**

- TOTAL FIXED COSTS **C10**, itself dependent on costs of RENT **C7** and TRANSPORT **C8**

will alter the profit or loss made and hence the breakeven point, i.e. the number of meals sold in order to just make a profit.

Facilities offered by most spreadsheet packages

All spreadsheet packages offer a wide range of facilities; some of the more important, and therefore more common ones, are summarized here.

- *Copying of equations* Having specified an equation or series of equations, these can then be copied from their source to any specified range within the spreadsheet. It is assumed, unless specified otherwise, that equation parameters (i.e. cell references) of copied formulae will change in line with the columns or rows to which they are copied. For a parameter to remain fixed and not to change relatively when copied it must be preceded by an **$** character. Hence, the previously specified profit/loss equation +E8*(C3 – C19) – C10 would, for copying purposes, have to be entered as

    +E8*(C$3 – C$19) – C$10

    since the equation parameters **C3**, **C19** and **C10** refer only to a single cell and must therefore be constrained, when copying vertically, not to change relative to the rows into which the original formula is to be copied.

- *Creating graphs* Up to a maximum of six variables can usually be plotted as:

    line graphs,

    bar charts,

    stacked-bar charts, and

    pie charts (one variable only)

    Figure 9 illustrates a composite diagram of these four principal graph types. Within a spreadsheet, graphs are dynamic in the sense that, if the numerical value of a defined variable alters, that same change is reflected in the related graph.

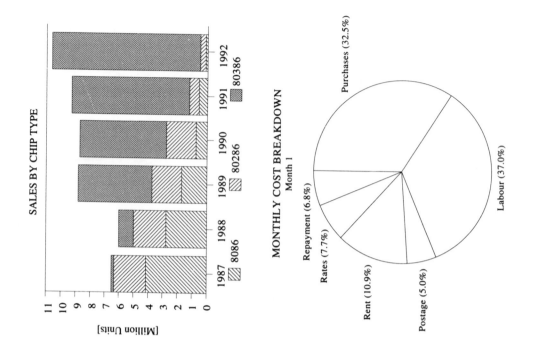

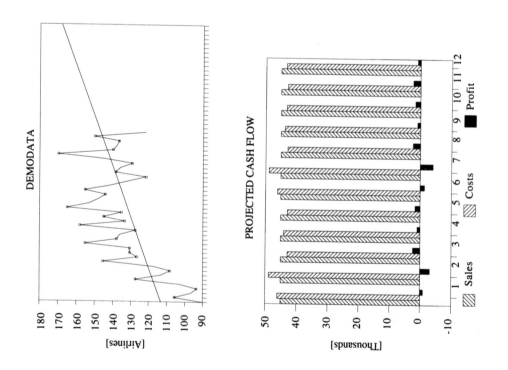

Figure 9 Typical spreadsheet graph types

- *Special functions* In addition to the standard arithmetic functions such as + (plus), - (minus), / (divide), * (multiply) and ^ (raise to the power), all spreadsheets contain a whole host of special functions (often more than one hundred), usually prefixed with the @ symbol.

  Some of the more common special functions are:

  @SUM( ) - summation over specified range

  @MAX( ) - detecting the maximum value over a specified range

  @ABS( ) - evaluating the absolute value

  @AVG( ) - evaluating the average value of a range

  @STD( ) - evaluating the standard deviation of a range

Historical background to the development of spreadsheet packages: Developed by Bricklin and a programmer colleague Robert Frankston, the first spreadsheet package VisiCalc (Visible Calculator) was launched in the late 70s on the early Apple II, Commodore and Tandy microcomputers with their uniquely different RAM-based operating systems. The conversion of VisiCalc to run in the first disk-based operating system environment, namely CP/M, in 1980-81 was delayed by legal wrangles. This led to a new package, SuperCalc, scooping the spreadsheet market — only to be replaced in its turn by Lotus 1-2-3 when PC/MS DOS became the predominant operating system for microcomputers with the introduction of the IBM PC to the UK in 1983. Subsequently, in spite of the introduction of many competitor spreadsheet packages to this most lucrative software market, Lotus 1-2-3 has continued to dominate the UK (and world) marketplace. SuperCalc spent most of the 1980s as a distant second, but has now slipped to third behind Microsoft's Excel, which has gained ground with the spread of the Windows environment. Other packages such as Quattro Pro, etc. have to attempt to increase their market share by offering even better facilities than the market leaders (or at least claiming to). In the current market, this is a classic example of the old adage about running at top speed just to stand still, since facilities are improving so rapidly.

3.2 Database packages (1)

Although there is no doubt that the spreadsheet package is the most common microcomputer applications package that any individual business user is likely to use personally, in terms of actual, routine applications, especially on large mainframe machines, the database package is more common. Indeed, one of the main responsibilities of the data processing department is to maintain the integrity of the company's main database(s) (see section 9).

In virtually all industrial and business organizations, files of records (i.e. a simple database) will be held of:

- Personnel — their personal details together with method of payment (see sections 3.26 and 3.25e)

- Stock items — their details together with transaction information of issues and receipts (see section 3.25d)

- Customers — their details together with financial information in terms of billings sent and payments received (sales ledger — see section 3.25a)

- Suppliers — their details together with financial information in terms of invoices received and payments made (purchase ledger — see section 3.25b)

All the databases, or to be more accurate, database *packages* described above are designed to meet particular applications and are characterized by being:

- inflexible in their design, in that the record structures are fixed and cannot be altered

- standardized, in the sense that most such databases will be accessed solely through a menu-driven interface designed only to allow pre-specified transactions with the information held in the database to be made.

Because standardized database applications are common and apply to most enterprises, the market for such packages is obviously large and it is worthwhile for professional software houses to develop such menu-driven, specialized packages. Even relatively small segments within this market may contain enough businesses to justify a specific development; for example, there is more than one database package available which specifically addresses the needs of dealers in the motor trade.

However, for the one-off database application on a personal computer, where the market is so small that it is clearly not worthwhile for professional software houses to develop such packages, the **flexible** database applications package, by providing alternative facilities such as:

- a flexible record structure, in the sense that the record structure can be designed by the user and subsequently modified if required

- a flexible user interface, in the sense that commands or menu choices formulated by the user can be used to extract information from the database in the form the user requires

represents a significant market sector in its own right.

Microcomputer-based, flexible database applications packages can be either *command* or *menu* driven, or a combination of the two. In a menu-driven package, the user gives instructions to the computer system by selecting from a menu of choices. A menu-driven package is usually easier to use, particularly for the beginner, but for the experienced user the necessary progression through a series of menus can be tedious.

In a command-driven package, the user types in commands to gain the required response; this therefore requires a knowledge of the package's command language on the part of the user. Hence, familiarization with a command-driven package is more difficult than for a menu-driven package, but as recompense a command-driven package is usually quicker in its response to the user's requirements.

One of the major advantages of a command-driven database package is that commands normally typed in as individual instructions can also be assembled in the form of statements within a program, thus permitting the design of menu-driven, bespoke systems using the package's command structure as a 'high-level language' (usually of the third but sometimes of the fourth generation; see section 2). Because the market for developing such systems is relatively large, the originating software houses have for some time provided *developer* versions of their product which enable them to produce so-called run-time systems. These allow developers to 'compile' completed systems that will then run for their clients without those clients being required to purchase the full version of the supporting flexible database package.

Ashton Tate's database package dBASE II, launched in the early eighties, was one of the first database packages with a command structure that could be used for programming purposes. Written originally by Wayne Ratcliff and Jeb Long of the Jet Propulsion Laboratory in Pasedena, California as a database programming language JPLDIS and marketed only by mail order through computer hobbyist magazines as a package known as VULCAN (a disproportionately large number of computing people are Star Trek fans), it was not until the marketing skills of the late George Tate were brought to bear that dBASE became the leading force in the personal computer database package world

The dBASE 'language' has now been adopted as the *de facto* standard within the microcomputer software industry, but even with a product line of dBASE III, dBASE III+ and currently dBASE IV offering ever increasing facilities, so competitive is the marketplace that Ashton Tate were hard pushed to maintain their market lead. Perhaps as a result, dBASE has now been taken over by Borland, who also produce one of its competitors, Paradox. Companies such as Fox Software, who originally produced a *superior* dBASE III+ clone Foxpro but have now broken from the dBASE mould and developed a package with a style of its own, along with many others offer products which challenge the market leader. Yet another potential market leader is DataEase, which has a reputation for being true to its name because of its heavy use of menus and prompted data entry screens.

Because within the flexible database package market products vary considerably in terms of command/menu structure, method of storing records and other facilities offered, prices vary from below £100 for a simple record holding system to over £500 for a comprehensive database package offering a complete set of database facilities.

3.3 Database packages (2)

Database vocabulary

As with most areas of expertise, the topic of computerized database applications has its own specialized vocabulary. In particular, the levels of information within a database system are described here and shown in illustrative form in Figure 10.

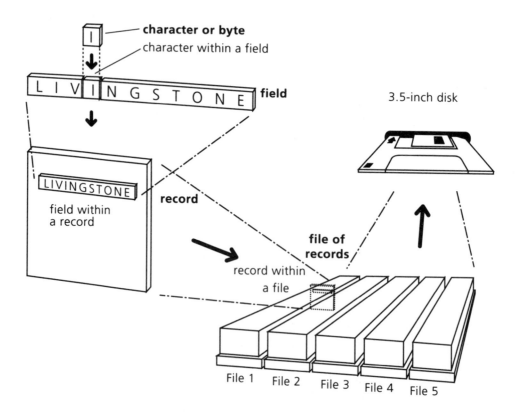

Figure 10 Levels of information within a database: several characters make a field, fields a record, records a file, files saved on disk.

CHARACTERS

The character is the lowest form of information in any database system, the twenty-six alphabet characters A to Z and the ten numeric characters 0 to 9 being the most commonly used, although some specialized characters are used in addition to these, for example the dollar sign $ and the underline or underscore _.

FIELDS

A collection or group of characters is referred to as a field which requires:

- a *Name* — which characterizes the type of data to be held, hence NAME (for surname), FNAME (for forename), etc. In a flexible database package it is the user who defines the names of fields.

- a *Type* — which defines the acceptable field contents. Common types include the following:

  numeric — which is restricted to the numeric characters 0 to 9, the decimal point (.) and the plus (+) and minus (–) signs, and on which simple arithmetic manipulations such as totalling, sub-totalling, etc. can be performed,

  character or **alphanumeric** — which is normally restricted to alphanumeric information of limited length, but when unrestricted may be referred to as a **text** field. *Alphanumeric* refers to one of the set consisting of A to Z, 0 to 9 and those special characters which that database package will accept as part of a 'word'. A source of considerable annoyance to those with hyphenated names is that many database packages will not accept a hyphen (-) as an alphanumeric character, so that for example the surname Harris-Jones must be stored as Harris_Jones, Harris Jones or, even worse, HarrisJones! Another source of confusion is that the numbers 0 to 9 as alphanumeric characters (effectively labels) are seen by the package as different from the same numbers as numeric characters (when they 'really are' numbers); this is another hangover from punched-card and paper-tape days.

  logical — which is restricted to one character such as Y (for yes) and N (for no) or M (for male) and F (for female),

  date — which usually has to be in a specified format such as dd/mm/yy (European) or mm/dd/yy (USA). Simple date arithmetic such as evaluating the difference between two dates (useful for identifying overdue bills!) can be performed.

- a *Width* — which specifies the maximum number of characters that can be contained. Field widths are specified by the user and in a flexible database package can be altered subsequently. For numeric fields with two decimal places it is advisable to be generous with field widths, particularly when totals and sub-totals are involved, since the two decimal places, the decimal point character (.) itself and the possible preceding + or - sign together represent four characters, and the result of a totalling process could represent another two. (NOTE: some flexible database packages are based on a fixed record size, in line with the user's specification of field widths. These fixed record length packages require the same amount of disk space for every record held irrespective of the amount of information contained in each record. Other, more sophisticated packages are based on flexible record sizes and only require disk space for actual information recorded.)

- the *Contents*, the actual information held within a field, i.e. the five characters **L E W I S** representing the contents of a character or alphanumeric type field named as Surname. Generally the contents of fields will be different for different records but even should two records appear identical in terms of field contents, they will still possess different, unique record numbers, as allocated by the package being used.

Figure 11 indicates the various properties of a field within a database.

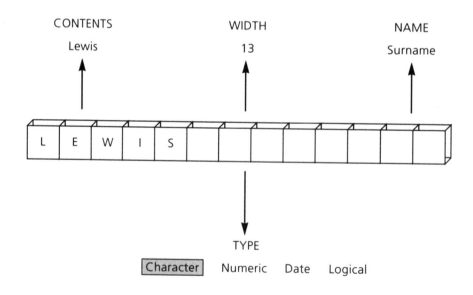

Figure 11 Properties of a field within a database

RECORDS

A record is a collection of fields. The number, type and size of fields within a record define the record structure, a typical example of which is shown as Figure 12 for a small, personnel database called STAFF. In this example the record structure is based on just five fields, four of which are character fields (COMPANY, DIV, DEPT and NAME) and one of which is numeric (SALARY). The size of each record is clearly a function of the total number of characters that could be accommodated by all field width specifications which, in this case, comes to 20 + 9 + 6 + 13 + 6 = 54 to which an extra character is added to act as an end-of-record marker. For a flexible database package based on a fixed record length, each record in this database would occupy 55 characters of disk space. Multiplying this by the number of records would give users a very rough indication of the disk space that will be required to hold the complete database.

Structure for database	: C:staff.dbf		
Number of data records	: 13		
Date of last update	: 07/28/93		
Field	Field name	Type	Width	Dec
1	COMPANY	Character	20	
2	DIV	Character	9	
3	DEPT	Character	6	
4	NAME	Character	13	
5	SALARY	Numeric	6	
** Total **			55	

Figure 12 The STAFF database

One of the big advantages of a flexible database package is that the record structure is initially specified by the user and can be modified subsequently. Thus if additional fields are required, these can be added to the record structure at any stage. Equally if fields need to be increased in width, these modifications can also be implemented at a later stage.

Although there is a technical limit to the number of fields that can be contained within a record, this is usually so high as not to cause a problem to the average user. However, with the limited display facilities usually provided by such packages, more than twenty fields per record are difficult to display within a single screen display for ease of interpretation.

Records in a database are normally held in record number order (referred to as *un-indexed*) and therefore are presented in the chronological order in which they were added to the database. Hence, in an un-indexed database, records would be listed in numerical order of record number (#) and would appear as shown in Figure 13, which is again from the database STAFF. In practice records will generally be displayed to the user *indexed* by whatever field (or combination of fields) is appropriate (see the sub-section on Indexing records in Appendix 3).

Database: STAFF   Page 1

#	COMPANY	DIV	DEPT	NAME	SALARY
1	UK MICRO	HOME	MKTG	JONES W	27000
2	EURO MICRO	EXPORT	PROD	THOMAS P J	24750
3	UK MICRO	EXPORT	R & D	BRYANT P	24000
4	EURO MICRO	HOME	PROD	YOUNGER W	18000
5	EURO MICRO	EXPORT	MKTG	LITTLE J	25250
6	UK MICRO	EXPORT	PROD	ABRAHAMS B R	21450
7	UK MICRO	HOME	MKTG	PARMAR B	24750
8	EURO MICRO	EXPORT	R & D	SHIRES S	26100
9	UK MICRO	EXPORT	MKTG	LEWIS C	27000
10	EURO MICRO	HOME	PROD	EDWARDS J	25600
11	EURO MICRO	HOME	PROD	GRANT B	22500
12	EURO MICRO	EXPORT	MKTG	LOESER G	19180
13	UK MICRO	EXPORT	PROD	GAGARIN Y	19000
14	EURO MICRO	HOME	R & D	BUNNAG A	28500
15	EURO MICRO	HOME	R & D	SOHAL D S	22000

Figure 13 Database records listed un-indexed

FILES

A collection of identically structured records can be defined as a simple (or *flat*, because it is two-dimensional) database and such records will be stored in a file. Although most packages have a technical limit on the number of records that may be held in such a file, in practice it is usually either the speed of the microcomputer or its storage capacity which limits the effective number of records.

As a reminder to the reader, the vocabulary of database terminology was shown previously as Figure 10 which illustrates the physical interpretation of the levels of information in a database namely, in ascending order:

CHARACTER,

FIELD,

RECORD, and

FILE (or DATABASE)

Selecting and counting records

Selecting (or searching for) records which meet a specified search criterion is one of the main facilities offered by a computerized database. Such searches cannot reasonably be done with a manual recording system when a large number of records is involved. Often linked with the selection procedure is the count facility which indicates how many records meet the search criterion. For both searching or counting the search criterion can be relatively simple, such as:

- all personnel in a certain department;
- all personnel earning above a certain salary;

or made more complex by use of logical AND or OR conjunctions, hence:

- all personnel in a certain department AND earning above a certain salary.

Examples of three such searches using these criteria as applied to the personnel database shown in Figure 13 are shown collectively in Figure 14.

When searching large databases, it is often sensible to count the number of records which meet a search criterion before listing the record contents. This is standard practice, for example, when doing literature searches on a bibliographic database in a library. This prevents unnecessary expense and/or the production of masses of unwanted hard-copy printout which, once started, cannot usually be stopped. If such a count reveals that too many records meet the search criterion, then by adding further conditions the initial criterion can be modified until the desired degree of selectivity is achieved.

Database: STAFF   Page 1

DEPT = "MKTG"

COMPANY	DIV	DEPT	NAME	SALARY
UK MICRO	HOME	MKTG	JONES W	27000
EURO MICRO	EXPORT	MKTG	LITTLE J	25250
UK MICRO	HOME	MKTG	PARMAR B	24750
UK MICRO	EXPORT	MKTG	LEWIS C	27000
EURO MICRO	EXPORT	MKTG	LOESER G	19180

Database: STAFF   Page 1

SALARY>25000

COMPANY	DIV	DEPT	NAME	SALARY
UK MICRO	HOME	MKTG	JONES W	27000
EURO MICRO	EXPORT	MKTG	LITTLE J	25250
EURO MICRO	EXPORT	R & D	SHIRES S	26100
UK MICRO	EXPORT	MKTG	LEWIS C	27000
EURO MICRO	HOME	PROD	EDWARDS J	25600
EURO MICRO	HOME	R & D	BUNNAG A	28500

Database: STAFF   Page 1

DEPT = "MKTG" AND SALARY>25000

COMPANY	DIV	DEPT	NAME	SALARY
UK MICRO	HOME	MKTG	JONES W	27000
EURO MICRO	EXPORT	MKTG	LITTLE J	25250
UK MICRO	EXPORT	MKTG	LEWIS C	27000

Figure 14 The results of three database searches

Conclusion

Flexible database packages offer a wealth of facilities which can be used to:

- create database files whose record structure is under the control of the user rather than prescribed by the originating software designer

- append or modify record structures at any stage, thus accommodating changing requirements for information needs

- search for, or count the number of, records in a database which meet a search criterion expressed in terms of a key

- organize the order in which records are presented to the user; either indexed on a single field or a combination of fields

- produce printed reports which can be either detailed or summary in form.

Examples of companies using flexible database packages and the purposes to which they have been put are:

- The Metropolitan Police have chosen the database package INGRES to link together a number of information systems. For such a large organization, independence of the hardware platform and operating system was a significant factor in this choice of software.

- The *Financial Times* chose the database package Empress to capture events reported from the London Stock Exchange to the FT Prices Room. The choice of Empress was mainly on speed of operation since real-time performance was paramount.

- The British Film Institute maintain a large database SIFT (Summary of Information on Film and Television) which has been designed specifically for hands-on use by non-computer experts. To run this system the BFI decided on the database package Adabas on grounds of speed and performance.

3.4 Graphics

Originally, computer graphics were very mathematically-based and not at all easy to use by non-mathematicians. The figures were constructed by drawing straight lines or arcs of a circle, and usually required an understanding of co-ordinate geometry to be used effectively. (*If you don't know what co-ordinate geometry is, don't worry — that serves to make our point.*) The breakthrough was a shift from a line-based approach to a shape-based approach, which fits in very well with a graphical user interface point-and-click style of operation (see section 1.2). This made it possible to choose (say) a rectangle, and simply stretch it to the right size and drag it to the right place, using just the mouse.

Figure 15 shows a simple example using the MacDraw package on an Apple Macintosh.

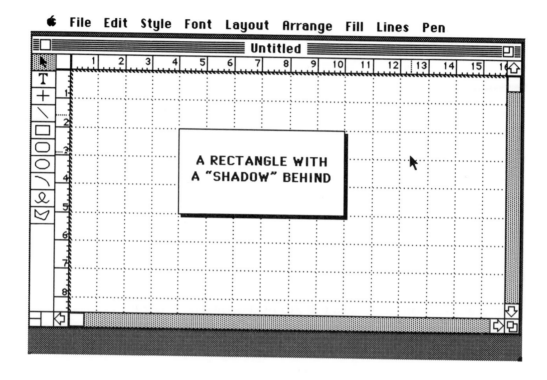

Figure 15 A graphics package in use

To this development was added the ability to convert tables of numbers into diagrams easily, whether they were graphs, histograms or pie charts, as linked to spreadsheets, and the geometrical knowledge required to produce impressive-looking diagrams was now minimal. Add to this the appearance of colour display screens, and more recently colour printers, for use with microcomputers, and you can see why the popularity of graphics packages has increased rapidly.

Apart from Computer-Aided Design (see section 3.19) and the production of diagrams for textbooks and articles, the major application of these techniques has been in producing slides for presentations and diagrams for brochures. Experiments at the Hawthorne School, one of the leading business schools in the USA, established that presentations supported by graphics are much more persuasive than those backed up by words alone. Any manager with access to a typical office personal computer can now use a package such as Harvard Graphics, Freelance or many others to dazzle his or her audience with multi-coloured diagrams. This idea, like many others in this world, is not without its snags. Believe it or not, the research results about graphics increasing the persuasiveness of a presentation do not actually apply to the comprehension of its content — presentation graphics are very much a tool for making an impression rather than creating an understanding: the 'gee-whizz' factor is very high!

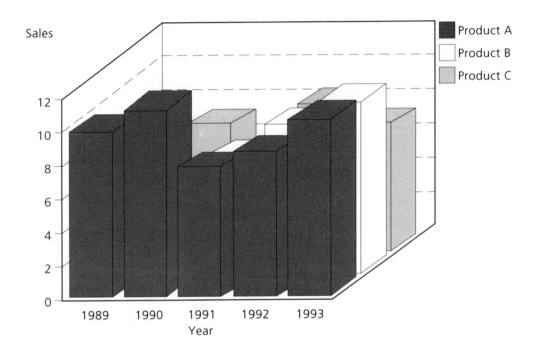

Figure 16 Graphics – 'How not to do it' (1)

A good example of this is the so-called three-dimensional bar chart, where perspective is used to add the illusion of depth to what would otherwise be a flat two-dimensional chart. Unfortunately, the 'three-dimensional' format often makes it very difficult to read across to the vertical scale and judge exactly how high the bars are. Even worse developments are the replacement of ordinary line graphs with ones in which the lines appear as the tops of 'solid walls'. This has the amusing feature that if several graphs are shown on the same set of axes, the top of one 'wall' for a low value can literally disappear down behind the walls in the foreground, so that the viewer cannot see it! Worst of all is the extension of circular pie-charts to sloping elliptical ones, where the whole point of the pie chart, namely that the size of the wedge represents the size of the figure being represented, is lost. Figures 16 and 17 give two examples of 'how not to do it'.

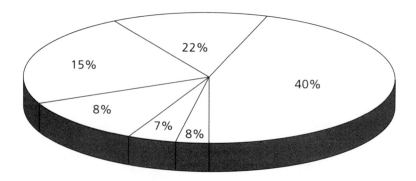

Figure 17 Graphics – 'How not to do it' (2)

Notwithstanding these criticisms, used in conjunction with a colour printer these packages are an excellent aid to sales and marketing staff, and to anyone else (including students) making presentations or producing reports. However, given that the tools may be used to mislead as well as to inform, a textbook such as the standard one by Edward R. Tufte[1] on the presentation of graphical information is more essential reading than ever.

Reference

1. Edward R. Tufte *The Visual Display of Quantitative Information*, Graphics Press, 1983.

3.5 Word-processing

If spreadsheets and databases are the most common personal software tools for the manager, the most commonly-used PC software package in business generally is the word-processing package. These packages evolved from the text editors which arrived at the time of interactive computing. Typing text into a computer raises problems on two levels. One is that of making mistakes in the typing, which need to be corrected; the other is that of deciding to change the text for 'editorial' reasons, i.e. to make the point of the text clearer for the reader. Allowing the user to correct typing mistakes is the essential basic function in an editor or word-processing package, but the better the facilities are for doing this, the more the package will be used for 'editorial' changes as well. Editors began by working with single lines of text at a time only (as if the text were still on punched cards), and gradually progressed to full-screen interactive editing with facilities to move the cursor around, 'cut' a block of text out from one place and 'paste' it back in again somewhere else, 'justify' the text (produce a straight edge on the right-hand edge of the page as well as the left) and so on, truly earning the name of 'word-processors'.

For example, correcting the same error which occurs in several different places (such as a spelling mistake in someone's name) is much easier with a 'search and replace' facility, permitting all the changes to be done in one operation. This made it possible to re-use letters, sending the same 'original' letter to different people, by doing a search for one name and replacing it with the other. This in turn led to the concept of a *standard letter*, containing all the text of the letter which is not to be personalized and is the same for all recipients, being linked to a database of names, addresses and even what are known in the trade as *salutations* or *greetings* (one can choose whether the letter begins 'Dear Captain Kirk' or 'Dear Jim'). Any database may be combined with any standard letter, as long as their structures match. This is called a *mail-merge* facility, and most modern word-processing packages will do this. Such personalized letters were the key to the expansion in the direct mailing industry during the 1980s, which is discussed further in section 3.29.

Current word-processing packages are able to incorporate elements such as graphs, charts, spreadsheets and even pictures produced by other packages. These developments led to desk-top publishing (DTP), dealt with later in section 3.18. With the constant addition of facilities and features to word-processing packages, the distinction between word-processing and DTP is not easy to define. Certainly a feature such as flowing text round a picture which only occupies part of a page, which belonged firmly to DTP a few years ago, is now virtually standard in WP. The latest word-processors nearly all offer the user the chance to see exactly what a complete page looks like as it will appear when printed, before actually printing it. This is known as 'wysiwyg' (What You See Is What You Get), pronounced 'whizzy-wig'. This may seem fairly trivial to do, but is actually quite difficult because most word-processing packages are character-based, in which each character takes up the same size 'slot' on the VDU no matter how large it is. It is much easier for the newer, graphics-based word-processors such as Ami Pro, where (for example) the letter w really is treated as being wider than the letter i.

The original microprocessor-based word-processors were actually dedicated machines, which pre-dated the main personal computer revolution; the authors can still remember using one with non-standard 8-inch diameter floppy discs. Nowadays, packages such as WordPerfect, Word, Wordstar and Ami Pro are available on PCs under all kinds of operating systems.

Perhaps the major advance in word-processing for those with limited keyboard skills has been the advent of the *spelling checker*, or *spell checker*. This is an electronically stored word-list, usually called a *dictionary*, although strictly this is not correct, as it stores only the words, not their meanings. It can be searched for every word you have typed, identifying those which do not appear (and thus may have been mis-spelt), and making suggestions as to correct spellings. The quality of these suggestions varies considerably between different spelling checkers, but in most cases the suggestions are far more effective if the first few letters of the word are correct. Most packages will suggest 'necessary' for 'necesary' or even 'neccessary', but if you type, say, 'salm' instead of 'psalm', the first suggestions are more likely to be 'sale' or 'salt'! Figure 18 shows the spelling checker in WordPerfect 5.1 at work on the previous sentence.

checkers, but in most cases the suggestions are far more effective if the first few letters of the word are correct. Most packages will suggest 'necessary' for 'necesary' or even 'neccessary', but if you type, say, 'salm' instead of 'psalm', the first suggestions are more likely to be 'sale' or 'salt'!

Doc 1 Pg 3 Ln 7.33" Pos 4.9"

A. necessary   B. necessaria

Not found: 1 Skip Once; 2 Skip; 3 Add; 4 Edit; 5 Look Up; 6 Ignore Numbers: 0

Figure 18 A spelling checker at work

An interesting point is that a larger dictionary does not always mean more effective checking of spelling. For example, 'manger' is a perfectly acceptable English word, but it is also a common mis-typing of 'manager'; in most businesses, except those dealing with Christmas carols and Christian publishing, it would probably be better to indicate 'manger' as a likely error. Most spelling checkers allow you to *add* words to the dictionary supplied, such as names and the technical jargon of your business, but none that we have used actually allows you to delete words from the dictionary.

It's worth remembering also that spelling checkers do not spot incorrect grammar; all of them will point out that 'thier' should be 'their', but whether it should really be 'there' is another issue altogether. There are one or two grammar and style checkers around, and some of the latest generation of word-processors include them, but they are less effective than the spelling checkers because there is less general agreement on what constitutes correct grammar, let alone correct style.

3.6 Electronic mail

The most basic of group computer tools is the electronic mail system, whereby different computer users can send messages to each other. Originally this began between different terminal users attached to the same machine, but gradually the facilities have extended to include communication between machines all the way from large mainframes down to personal computers.

It has often been claimed that the growth of electronic mail would lead to the 'paperless office', but so far there appear to be few signs of this happening. Some organizations however, notably IBM (who could be accused of having a vested interest), have succeeded in completely replacing their paper-based internal memo system by one based on electronic mail.

Originally, electronic mail (e-mail) was restricted to terminal-based systems; the first proprietary e-mail packages therefore came, not surprisingly, from the major vendors of hardware for mainframe and mini-computer systems, such as IBM's PROFS and Digital's All-In-One. As personal computer networks have become more common, so e-mail packages designed for them have also appeared, often from the leading software houses such as Microsoft Mail and Lotus cc:Mail. Many packages now operate on both personal computers and larger systems, for example IBM's OfficeVision and ICL's OfficePower.

Effectively, electronic mail packages offer a range of facilities for creating, sending, reading and storing messages. It is now standard practice to send e-mail messages across the world in both business and academia, using networks such as JANET and Internet (see section 14.1). Public e-mail systems also exist, such as BT Mailbox Service (formerly Telecom Gold) and Mercury Messaging in the UK.

Advocates of e-mail have been known to claim that it combines all the advantages of writing a letter and making a telephone call. This is clearly an exaggeration, but it does have several distinct benefits, as we shall see in this section as we compare 'ordinary paper mail', e-mail, telephone and that other technology which appeared in the 1980s, fax (facsimile), as means of business communication.

Table 8 Comparison of different methods of business communication

PAPER MAIL	ELECTRONIC MAIL
Advantages	*Advantages*
Universal	Quick (but not instant)
Read and write when convenient	Multiple copies as easy as one
Legally acceptable	Instant filing
	Read and write when convenient
	Know when it has been read
Disadvantages	*Disadvantages*
Slow (may never arrive at all)	Not everyone has it
Don't know if it has been read	Effectively text only
Not interactive	Not fully interactive
Takes time to produce	Legally unacceptable
TELEPHONE	FAX
Advantages	*Advantages*
Interactive	Instant
Instant	Text plus graphs, maps etc.
Allows more freedom of expression	Legally acceptable
Disadvantages	*Disadvantages*
Other person has to be there	Not everyone has it
Not everyone has it	Slow to send long document
Legally difficult to substantiate	Not interactive

Table 8 summarizes the advantages and disadvantages of the different methods. From this it can be seen that the 'best of both worlds' claims for electronic mail are based on the fact that it avoids the main disadvantages of paper mail and the telephone, in that it arrives quickly, the other person does not have to be there at the moment it is sent, and it is possible for the sender to know when the recipient has read it. This latter feature is achieved by attaching a *Read receipt* to the e-mail message, which automatically sends an e-mail message back to the sender when the recipient reads the original message. Initially this feature was only available within an organization, but now it is possible in some cases to extend this to e-mail to and from other organizations.

Note however that some systems now allow the recipient to *prevent* this facility from being used on messages sent to him/her, on the grounds that it may be an invasion of the recipient's privacy for the sender to know the exact time when the message was read! (*How would you feel about that in the case of an urgent e-mail message from your boss, for example?*)

E-mail does also have the key advantages associated with the use of computers that it is almost as easy to send a message to multiple recipients as it is to one, and that messages can be filed instantly. Computer-linked fax machines are, however, beginning to offer facilities in this area which are nearly as good. Perhaps the key disadvantages of e-mail at present in a business context are:

- Not everyone has it; remember many of an organization's communications are to the general public, not to other companies.

- In the UK and in most other countries, the legal status of e-mail messages, for example in contractual matters, is, to say the least, questionable. This is not specific to e-mail, but rather the general problems which the law has had in coming to grips with the status of computer-generated and computer-stored documents as evidence.

From the business manager's point of view, it is also worth remembering that e-mail and the telephone have the advantages of being available 'at the desk', whereas for most managers sending a letter or a fax requires just a little more effort and (for those fortunate enough still to have one) the involvement of a secretary or typist as well.

From the organization's point of view, it has been claimed that the use of electronic mail tends to overcome traditional hierarchical 'boundaries' to communication, permitting a 'flatter' and better-connected organizational structure, and a more responsive organization. On the other hand, if e-mail replaces face-to-face meetings, as some have suggested it can, then there is an increased chance of misunderstandings arising from the limited amount of expression which e-mail allows.

Electronic communication technology will undoubtedly continue to improve at a rapid rate, with voice, video, text and graphics becoming more closely linked, but it will never replace the letter until everyone has access to the electronic systems.

3.7 Personal diaries

One of the symbols of the 1980s in the UK was the personal organizer book or Filofax. These were — and are – used to keep lists of appointments, reminders, names and addresses, and a host of other things. Computers can potentially also perform these functions very well, since all of them are basically for the storage and/or retrieval of information. Indeed, computer-based diaries have considerable advantages, ranging from inserting regular appointments such as the weekly sales team meeting on Fridays at 2 pm, to automatically dialling telephone numbers from the address book (providing your computer is connected to the 'phone, of course!). Thus it was not long before the personal computer had its personal organizer package for you to use on the PC in your (personal?) office. Unfortunately, this was its limitation — it wasn't a great deal of use if you were not *in* your office. They were however very successful as *home* computer packages (Apple Macintosh computers in the late 1980s came with free software which included a personal organizer), and made a further advance in the business market when these facilities became available to groups of people with the networking of personal computers. The importance of the last point is that one of the most annoying tasks in business is trying to arrange meetings; this is much easier if the meeting organizer can have access to the diaries of everyone who is supposed to attend. When this is done electronically, searching for a suitable time-slot is made much more straightforward. Of course, this does raise issues of privacy similar to those we have already discussed in section 3.6; the normal compromise is that when you access someone else's diary, you can see when they are busy, but not what they are supposed to be doing.

The other breakthrough was once again an advance in hardware, which produced truly 'use anywhere' computers in the form of lap-top PCs; personal organizer packages then moved fully from the realm of gimmicks into that of useful business tools. Indeed, as even smaller computers have become available, a whole market has sprung up in calculator-sized *electronic organizers* (a name coined by Sharp, who are prominent in this market) where the diary and address-book software is permanently loaded in the computer. Personal diaries/electronic organizers also form one of the key functions for the new generation of hand-held, pen-input computers or PDAs (Personal Digital Assistants). Figure 19 shows a page from the electronic diary in the Apple Macintosh sofware mentioned earlier.

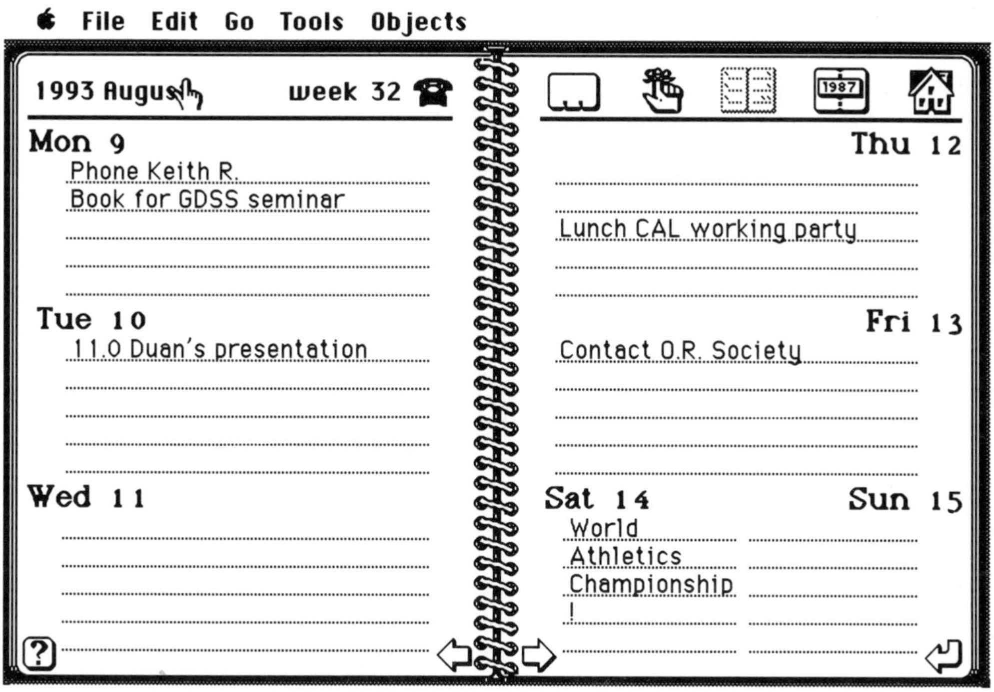

1993 August week 32 ☎

Mon 9
Phone Keith R.
Book for GDSS seminar

Tue 10
11.0 Duan's presentation

Wed 11

Thu 12

Lunch CAL working party

Fri 13
Contact O.R. Society

Sat 14   **Sun 15**
World
Athletics
Championship
!

Figure 19 An 'electronic' diary

3.8 Decision support systems

It could be argued that virtually all management information is intended to assist decision-making, and so the dividing line between decision support systems (DSS) and management information systems (MIS) is far from clear-cut. Different authors have different views on this point, and there is no proper consensus about the distinction (if any) between the two.

A more specific description of DSS than most is the 'working definition' given by Efraim Turban in his book[1] (p.73): 'A DSS is an interactive CBIS (*computer-based information system*) that utilizes decision rules and models coupled with the decision-maker's own insights, leading to specific, implementable decisions in solving problems that would not be amenable to management science optimisation models *per se*.' Note that Turban uses the term CBIS where we use MIS.

For the purpose of this book, decision support systems refer to systems intended to help the individual manager (or possibly a group of managers — see section 3.12), and management information systems to systems intended to support the organization as a whole. This of course isn't clear-cut either; the same system could be described as both a DSS and an MIS depending on the viewpoint from which it is being considered. However, we trust that the difference in focus is clear; DSS focus on supporting decision-making, MIS on producing information, usually in the form of reports.

A typical decision support system comprises three parts:

- a database
- a model base
- a user interface (sometimes called a *dialogue* subsystem).

The features of a *database* are described in the various Database Packages sections of this book. The database in the DSS may be created specifically for the DSS, or data may be obtained as required from other databases either internal or external to the organization.

The *model base* consists either of models which have already been constructed for the problems which the decision-maker faces, or of modelling tools with which he or she may build models to explore the problem(s). More details of what goes into the model base belong to the realms of operational research and management science, and are beyond the scope of this book; a suitable reference is Kidd[2].

The *user interface* of all computer systems needs careful consideration, but it is particularly important in the case of DSS. This is because DSS are designed to be used by managers, who are relatively senior in organizations, and in most cases have the choice as to whether they use the DSS or not. It is very difficult to force managers to take decisions in a particular way! Thus the user interface needs to be tailored to the preferences of the decision-maker concerned. Sprague and Carlson developed a framework for what needs to be taken into account in designing a DSS called the ROMC Approach. This stands for Representations, Operations, Memory Aids and Control Mechanisms.

- *Representations* should match the way the decision-maker thinks about the problem: if he/she uses a map, there should be a map on the screen (see section 3.28). Lists, graphs, reports and statistical analyses are other possibilities.

- What *operations* are to be done using the system? For example, gather data, generate reports, choose between alternatives.

- *Memory Aids* include databases, workspaces, triggers and flags such as exception reports, and special views.

- *Control Mechanisms* include menus, function keys, short-cuts, standard conventions, and even training of users!

Having looked at what needs to be taken into account, another way of looking at DSS is to consider the basic functions which the system carries out. The best-known work on this is by Steven Alter. Although it dates back to the late 1970s, not very long after the term decision support systems came into use, it is still widely accepted. This is because the credibility of Alter's seven categories (shown in Figure 20) was considerably enhanced by successfully anticipating two major developments in decision support which did not exist in commercial use at the time — spreadsheets and expert systems (see sections 3.1 and 3.11).

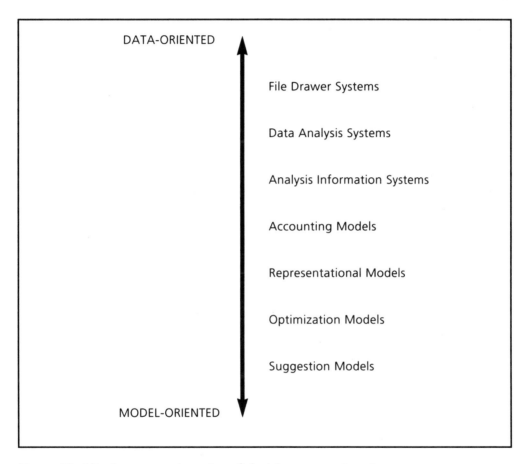

Figure 20 Alter's seven categories of decision support system

Alter's seven categories range from those where the emphasis is on the data, to those where the emphasis is on the model. Starting from the data-oriented end:

File drawer systems (a British researcher would have called them filing cabinet systems) are an automated version of a manual filing system, allowing access to data items. For example, a salesperson looking at the stock records to see if the item you want is available, a travel agent accessing an airline reservation system to see if a flight is fully booked, or a personnel manager retrieving the details of one of the company's employees.

Data analysis systems allow the general or specific manipulation of data, for example budget analysis according to account codes or selecting all students who failed a particular course. Most flexible database packages offer facilities for these operations (see sections 3.2 and 3.3).

Analysis information systems offer access to a series of databases rather than just one, generally including both internal company information and external information. They also have a limited modelling capability, usually just for forecasting. Marketing DSS typically come into this category.

Accounting models carry out calculations based on the standard accounting conventions. They are used for budgeting and financial planning, and to produce standard financial statements such as income and expenditure reports and balance sheets. They are also extensively used for 'what if?' analysis. This is the category into which the major use of spreadsheets fits.

Representational models are also used for predictive calculations, but this time based on more general models which typically include an element of uncertainty or risk. Examples include Monte Carlo simulation (see section 3.22), corporate modelling and risk analysis.

Optimization models carry out what is known in operational research circles as optimization under constraint, the best-known example of which is linear programming. The system calculates a solution to the model, which may then be used in the 'real world', either exactly or as a guideline.

Suggestion models, as their name implies, also suggest solutions, but unlike the previous category these solutions are based on rules of thumb rather than precise mathematical algorithms. Examples include 'scoring' systems for dealing with applications for credit, systems to work out insurance premiums and an example Alter gives of a system to price cardboard boxes. This is the category which foreshadowed the commercial use of expert systems.

Finally, we come to the components used to build the DSS. In hardware terms, the best system to use for delivering a DSS is the one which is already on the manager's desk! Increasingly this is a personal computer, though it may still be a terminal to a larger machine, or in rare cases a special-purpose workstation. The software used should be whatever suits the purpose of the DSS best and is available, although it is worth bearing in mind that various types of software ranging from spreadsheets to Fourth Generation Languages have been claimed as particularly suitable for DSS development. As with all computer system developments, the final choice of software should be able to be left to the technical specialists; the user should not have to worry about it.

DSS Examples

1. In the late 1970s and early 1980s, British Telecom developed various DSS for strategic modelling; these were based on the use of colour graphics at a time when this was technologically difficult and required a special-purpose workstation. Top management and corporate planners used the system to analyze the effect of government policy changes and environmental effects on BT, and also to look at both suppliers and customers in the market for communication services (defined very widely — even including newspapers). The inclusion in the model of a privatization option (even before the election of Mrs. Thatcher's government in 1979) helped to make it very successful!

2. British Airways use various DSS for human resource planning, including one which helps in 'grade re-structuring'. This is a common problem in large organizations because job grading systems tend to become out-dated. It combines a pay model based on typical spreadsheet facilities with the ability to download information from the mainframe personnel database; in addition there are routines to speed up the design of new grading systems and to perform 'stocks and flows' modelling of human resources.

3. DYANA: A marketing DSS based on market research information, provided by the Market Research Corporation of America (MRCA). This is the classic analysis information system. DYANA facilitates access to MRCA's customer purchase behaviour database. A market researcher in one of MRCA's client companies selects a customized working database from the main database to be downloaded to his or her PC, where they may then carry out various kinds of analysis such as repeat purchasing, brand switching or producing frequency distributions. This mode of operation means that MRCA maintains ownership of the data in the database; the user need not be aware of being connected to the mainframe at all — the PC can be set up to use an auto-dial facility to the MRCA database when necessary.

4. Heineken NV, the brewery based in the Netherlands, uses a plant-location DSS. In Alter's classification, this is an optimization model. Heineken frequently needs to consider plant-location and distribution problems, involving a hierarchy of 4 levels — plants, bottle lines, depot locations and customers. The model is used to analyze the effects of changing capacity and cost parameters (especially for the depots) and deals with both Dutch and foreign conditions. Since it involves 10 products, 20 production lines, 50 existing and potential depots and 1000 customers, the model includes no fewer than 50,000 variables!

References
1. E. Turban *Decision Support and Expert Systems: management support systems* (third edition), Macmillan, New York, 1993.
2. J. B. Kidd (ed.) *Managing with Operational Research,* Philip Allan, Deddington, 1985.

3.9 Data processing

Although data processing is perhaps the most basic of business computing activities, we shall not devote very much space to it in this book. The reason is not that it is unimportant; on the contrary, without effective data processing systems, most businesses would not be able to use any more sophisticated computer systems. Rather, the reason is that for most managers, data processing and its problems are 'invisible'; the province of the computing specialists and of large batch jobs chugging away in the small hours of the morning. This is a reasonable enough situation *as long as the managers do not take it for granted*. Like the electricity or water supply, people only tend to notice the data processing system when things go wrong!

Managers do not need to worry too much about the technical details, but they should remember why they need the system. In many cases, the data processing system is absolutely 'mission-critical' for the organization. For example, the banks are crucially dependent on their systems which process cheques and credits. When a person hands a cheque for their electricity bill over the counter at their branch, the systems *must* correctly debit the amount of that cheque from their account, and credit exactly the same amount to the electricity company's account; and do it within a stated period of time. Since the electricity company's account is likely to be with a different bank from that of the person paying the bill, at least three computer systems will be involved (one in each of the two banks, and one to 'exchange' the amount between them). Millions of these transactions have to be processed every day, although in fact 'every day' is a slight misnomer, as much of this processing is in fact done during the night when pressure on the banks' other systems is lower. Printing off the customers' bank statements is also typically done during the night; not only because the statements are then correct 'at close of business', but also because the printers have to be loaded with special stationery, and it therefore makes sense to do all the statements together. By contrast, ATM (Cashpoint) withdrawals have to be processed by the computer immediately, even if the account balance is not updated straightaway. A single bank's ATM system may have to deal with as many as 100 withdrawals per second at the peak time of the day (when people leave work in the evening).

Similar processing problems face other financial institutions, insurance companies, mail order firms, utilities, retailers — even the football pools companies preparing to computer-check their clients' entries against each Saturday's results. For example, the Automobile Association's two ICL mainframe computers process between 350,000 and 400,000 transactions each day. Again, while some of these, such as a change of address, update the database instantly, others, such as notifying the AA's underwriters of new insurance business taken on that day, are done in batches during the night.

As we have said, the technical issues should not concern the average manager, but the correct functioning of these systems may well be vital to the survival of the business (see Part D).

3.10 Management information systems

Once the early computerization of accounts, payroll and stock recording had been carried out, attention turned to other ways of using computers to make businesses more effective. It was apparent that any accounting or order-processing system could very easily produce summaries of information in various forms; not just standard accounting statements like balance sheets or profit and loss accounts, but summary reports tailored to the needs of a particular manager. Adding up totals, sorting items into order, retrieving certain items and calculating sub-totals for them, are all tasks which computers can do very well.

Building on these foundations produced the Management Information Systems (MIS) movement in the early 1960s. Remember that at that time there were no interactive systems in business (see the Introduction), and so the output of an MIS (or indeed any computer system) had to be in the form of a printed report. There were (and indeed still are) two basic types of report. One is a standard report produced at regular intervals, which might be anything from daily (for a list of stock items needing to be re-ordered that day) to yearly (for a summary of staff costs in different branches of an organization). The other is an *ad hoc* report, produced in response to a specific request.

In some ways the concept of MIS was a great advance. However, there were snags. Since this was often the first time that information had been provided to managers in this way, managers often found that the reports either contained far too much information for their needs, or that they still did not cover exactly the right information. This is in fact the major challenge of any information systems development: providing exactly the information which is required; no more, and no less. Unlike many things in life, too much information is just as much of a problem as too little. The influence of computers has generally been to shift the manager's problem from a lack of information to finding the relevant information. MIS clearly are not the answer to *all* management information problems, but their invention did successfully address some of them, especially where the ideal format of the report was already known, but the difficulty was providing timely information, i.e. producing the information quickly enough, as in the example of the list of items which need re-ordering.

The position of management information systems has been further improved with the advent of first interactive and then desktop systems, but in many cases the degree of interaction which a manager has with a large management information system is still limited to a choice of standard reports. This is not surprising, because many managers are understandably reluctant to have to learn how to specify *ad hoc* reports to the computer for themselves, despite the development of fourth-generation languages or 4GLs (see section 2) to make the process easier. In any case, interactive systems are not always superior to printed reports; a building society manager will probably find it easier to work with a printed list of clients who are more than six months in arrears with their mortgage payments than one on a VDU screen. So, because standard reports will always have a place in management monitoring and decision-making, MIS will continue to be used and useful. A newer development on the same theme is that of Executive Information Systems (see section 3.21), which take a different approach to the problem of specifying *ad hoc* reports by vastly increasing the range and format of the 'standard' reports which are available. These, as the name implies, are specifically aimed at the most senior executives, who form a relatively small proportion of the total number of managers in an organization. There are signs that the Executive Information Systems approach is beginning to percolate downwards in the organization, but it is clear that most management information requirements will continue to be met by management information systems for some while yet!

3.11 Expert systems

Expert systems are arguably the most successful commercial result of research into artificial intelligence (see section 3.16 for further discussion). The objective of developing an expert system is to match the performance of a human expert in a particular field of expertise. In expert systems terminology, this is called the *domain* of the expert system, and it has to be a very narrow one, or else the computer has (at present) no chance of matching the human's performance. So, the domain of the expert system might be to diagnose faults in a particular piece of equipment, or to recommend treatment for one kind of disease. Note that the expertise has to be intellectual rather than physical; that of the lawyer rather than the dentist!

What makes expert systems different from, say, spreadsheets or statistical packages is the nature of the expertise they try to capture. (After all, computer systems that can do calculations faster than human 'experts' have been around for nearly 50 years.) They differ in two ways.

First, expert systems attempt to represent the *heuristics*, the 'rules of thumb' which the human expert has acquired through years of training and experience in his or her specialized area. For example, a human medical consultant will have begun by studying basic sciences, then studied the theory behind medicine (to degree level), then begun to practise medicine, probably in a general area at first, and then gradually becoming recognized as being knowledgeable about a particular specialized area of medicine. Although much of the basic knowledge is available in books, the knowledge or expertise which establishes a consultant's reputation as an expert is not in the books, and can only be acquired 'on the job'.

Second, expert systems attempt to produce a result even when the available data are uncertain or incomplete. (A computer program designed for calculation will not function with incomplete data. At best, it will produce an error message or a request for the missing figure(s); at worst, a meaningless result.)

The idea overall is to produce a result based on judgement rather than calculation. The use of the word 'expert' in this context has led to a few problems. Some of the expertise in DENDRAL, the first expert system, did indeed come from a Nobel prize-winner, but expertise does not need to be at such a high level in order to be useful. In the appropriate context, a merchant bank's top investment advisor and the person in the mail room who knows the best way to send a parcel to Hong Kong to arrive by Monday may both possess scarce expertise. Indeed, for many of the tasks for which this type of computer system appears to be useful, the term expert system seems somewhat pretentious. Knowledge-based system is probably a more accurate description, but the phrase 'expert system' is more common.

Examples of expert systems

1. VATIA This is a system developed in the UK by what was then Ernst & Whinney, now part of Ernst & Young, one of the largest accounting and financial consultancy organizations. It was designed to help Ernst & Whinney's general auditors assess the adequacy and compliance with legislation of clients' Value Added Tax (VAT) systems and procedures. (VAT is a tax levied on supplies of goods and services, and thus a major concern of most organizations in the UK and indeed Western Europe.) The auditors have some knowledge of VAT, but are not themselves 'experts' in the field; the expertise was provided by Ernst & Whinney's VAT specialists. The VATIA system was installed on all the portable microcomputers used on audit assignments. Some 600 copies had been installed by May 1988.

2. STOCKMASTER This is an expert system developed by two Swedish companies: Traversum AB, a company specializing in the stock market, and Novacast Expert Systems AB (expert systems specialists, as their name implies). It is designed to evaluate an individually quoted stock or future valuation, with a view to a recommendation to buy, hold or sell. The system has been in daily use by Traversum AB since January 1987.

3. POLAPRES This system was developed by Metallurgique et Minière de

Rodange-Athus (MMRA), a steel-making company based in Luxembourg. It diagnoses faults in the process of rolling, in which heated ingots of steel are passed through large cylindrical presses. It was developed with the twin aims of preserving the expertise of MMRA's principal rolling 'expert', who was due to retire, and of reducing the number of calls on the experts during the night shift. It has been in use (by the 'non-expert' manufacturing foremen) since mid-1987. By now the system has more than repaid the development costs of some $235,000; this figure includes the considerable amount of work needed to produce the original non-expert system record of all the defects which might arise during steel rolling at MMRA.

4. AUTHORIZER'S ASSISTANT American Express commissioned this system to help with the task of authorizing credit card transactions — over one million such transactions take place per month. A major element in constructing the system was interfacing the expert system, running on a workstation, with American Express's existing transaction processing and database systems, running on mainframes.

5. XCON (originally R1) Almost certainly the most commercially successful expert system is the XCON system, used by Digital Equipment Corporation (DEC). It configures computer systems, taking the customer's order and producing a series of diagrams showing the hardware components in the system and how they are to be put together, for the technician who physically assembles the system. It has now been in use since 1980, and the DEC executive responsible for the original R1 project was quoted in 1987 as claiming that it had saved the company $40 million in that year alone. Much of this figure was accounted for by the belief that it would have been impossible for the company to have continued its stated policy of tailoring systems to customer requirements without the expert system.

Differences between expert systems and more conventional computer systems

Perhaps the most important difference between expert systems and more conventional computer systems is that most organizations of medium size and above have quite a lot of experience of developing and using conventional computer systems, but relatively few have significant experience of expert systems and fewer still have experience of large expert systems.

Despite this, or perhaps even because of it, a common reaction from many data processing professionals when they encounter an expert system for the first time is: 'This is no different from what I do already.' To some extent this is certainly true — at the level of program modules, there is little to distinguish an expert system from a conventional computer system written in the same language. However, both the nature of the systems and the way in which they fit into the operations of the organization are likely to differ substantially.

Among the differences which can be identified are the following:

- The technology used in typical data processing (DP) applications is well established; there is little doubt as to whether it is actually *possible* to build a computer system for that application. This is not the case with the present state of development of the expert system field.

- Involvement of high-level managers or non-computing technical specialists in the actual *building* of a DP system (as opposed to its commissioning or specification) is rare. The nature of an expert system makes the close involvement of one or more domain experts almost inevitable.

- As the tasks for which an expert system is suitable are often inherently more complex than those which a DP system can perform, the user interface normally has to be correspondingly more sophisticated.

- It is extremely difficult, and sometimes impossible, to specify the performance objectives of an expert system in the way that is advocated for DP systems. This has implications both for estimating the resources required to develop the system, and for the extent to which prototyping is likely to be required as part of the system development process.

- The fact that expert systems typically contain judgements and rules of thumb, which are *not* correct 100% of the time, may cause problems in the way in which people react to the system and its uses — apart from the practical problems it poses for system testing.

One final difference is in terms of the ease of replacing a non-computer system with a computer-based one. In a traditional data processing application, the manual procedures are often explicitly set out. There is thus little uncertainty as to what the task itself entails, and the computer system could be based on a straightforward step-by-step 'translation' of the old manual system. (N.B. We are saying it *could* be, not that it *should* be!)

However, where an expert system is suitable, it is most unlikely that the required knowledge or expertise will have been written down, or made explicit in any other usable form.

A simple example of a 'chunk' of expertise

Often what distinguishes knowledge or expertise from information is the way in which it is written down or made available. A typical user guide to a piece of computer software is arranged in terms of the functions of the various commands; similarly, a hardware manual is likely to be arranged according to what the switches on the printer or the keys on the keyboard do. Yet often we actually need to retrieve that information, i.e. *use* the expertise, in a way which is based on the context in which the system is being used. The question to be answered is: 'I want to do this — how do I do it?' or 'This is happening/not happening — what do I do?'

So, for example, although the manual tells you the circumstances in which the keyboard on your terminal has no effect (if you know where to look!), in order to have any usable expertise you need to be able to access it in the form of 'rules' like the following:

IF the user is a novice

AND the user is complaining that nothing appears on the screen when the keys are pressed

THEN the No Scroll key is probably pressed down.

Some of the better manuals these days do indeed have fault-finding sections written with this type of emphasis, but they are much harder to write than a conventional manual because of the fuzziness of the context in which difficulties arise about how to carry out tasks compared to the technical specification of what the system is supposed to do. It is probably no coincidence that it is only since the widespread appearance of expert systems that the importance of trying to write down, or otherwise 'record', information on how to perform a task has been realized. (See also the discussion in Programming Languages section 2.)

3.12 Group decision support systems

Group decision support is concerned with people making decisions *as a group*. Thus group decision support systems (GDSS) add two extra dimensions to 'ordinary' decision support systems:

● Supporting communications between members of the group

● Helping the group to make a decision, by achieving consensus, or at least an agreed compromise.

The second of these may include systems for voting on or ranking alternative courses of action, for example.

Many authors believe that the GDSS itself should contain mechanisms which discourage negative group behaviour such as destructive conflict, miscommunication or 'group-think'. Others, however, feel that this laudable aim is not always easy to achieve in practice, partly because the presence of the GDSS may affect the behaviour of the group members.

The basic activities to be supported by group decision support systems are information retrieval, information sharing and information use.

Information retrieval has two basic components: data from databases, and opinions and attitudes from other group members.

Information sharing may be among the group as a whole, or to/with selected individuals. The possibilities for this may be affected by the physical environment in which the decision is being made (see below).

Information use consists of 'typical' DSS-type modelling, plus group problem-solving procedures. The latter include activities such as brainstorming as well as the voting or ranking mentioned above.

Hardware

In group decision support, there must be the means to communicate between individuals and the control of shared resources, such as a big display screen which everyone present can look at at the same time. The first requires either networking of the individual computers, or that everyone work with terminals to a host machine; the former of these is now much more common. The second almost always means the presence of a person acting as *group facilitator* in addition to the decision-makers.

An alternative approach addressing both of these issues is to have only one computer, which all members must share, with perhaps another machine for the exclusive use of the facilitator. The intention of this is to encourage face-to-face communication and the sharing of information amongst the whole group.

It may be either necessary or desirable to use an input device which is simpler (or at least less obtrusive) than the standard QWERTY keyboard. The *keypad,* a device like a TV remote control, with numeric keys plus one or two others, has found some success in practical use, especially where there is a single shared computer.

Software

Mostly the software needed will be the same as a combination of good individual DSSs, with an emphasis on graphics. Spreadsheet and database software would now be expected as standard. In addition, facilities will be needed for displaying preferences, judgements, the results of votes, etc.

The scenario

Most work on GDSS assumes that the decision is made with all the decision-makers in the same place, a *decision room*. The phrase *decision conference* is also used for this setting. As well as the computing equipment, it will in addition be necessary to include slide and video display equipment, and perhaps even the facility for 'good old flip charts' and so on.

There has been a little work on GDSS in which the group members remain in their own offices, but most workers in the field feel that a decision room is essential, in order to avoid the loss of face-to-face as well as 'through the machine' communication. An interesting contrast is between the *computer-based* type of decision room, generally laid out as a set of personal computers, perhaps in a U-shape, and the *group-centred* type of room, where the technology is hidden behind the walls.

Purpose-built decision rooms with a computer for each participant are expensive. Probably the best-known successful example of one in a commercial company is that in use at the Boeing Aircraft Corporation in the USA. A few consultancies and universities have set up decision rooms which may be rented by organizations when necessary, for example those at ICL and the London School of Economics. The single shared computer approach thus has considerable financial attractions, since most organizations do have a meeting room or board room already, and so the group facilitator only needs to bring one or two computers.

3.13 Computer-aided learning

Computer-aided learning (CAL) is widely used in both industry and education, as a means of delivering 'individual' instruction to large numbers of people. It has perhaps been most successful in teaching skills and procedures, such as how to fill in a particular type of form, what to do in a certain set of circumstances, or indeed how to use a particular computer software package; in the skills context it is often referred to as computer-based training, or CBT. CAL/CBT was originally the logical development of programmed-learning books. These are still in existence today. The student's path through the book is determined by answers to questions on the material being learnt ('if your answer is A, turn to page 12, if your answer is B, turn to page 15'). The same approach is used in various series of 'make your own adventure' books covering detective stories, 'sword and sorcery', etc.

A computer-based system has the obvious advantage over a book that it is much less likely that the student will turn to the wrong 'page' by accident. However, CAL systems can go much further than this. An early example was the replacement of a fixed set of questions by specially generating the questions each time, either by selecting from a database or (for certain mathematical topics) by producing completely random numbers. This made it possible for a student to use the same CAL module several times without either becoming bored stiff or learning the right answers off by heart, 'parrot-fashion'. In addition, the system can automatically record the students' answers, both to evaluate their individual performances, and for the instructors to see which parts of the material students are finding difficult, and so on.

As the capabilities of computer systems have improved, it has become possible to add graphics and sound capabilities to the CAL material, and even to allow free-format answers, rather than simply multiple-choice selection. The latter is made possible by rapid database searching techniques. The parts of the system dealing with the explanation of the material (rather than the testing of the student's knowledge) have also been greatly improved by the use of hypertext (see section 3.17). This gives the student much more control over the order in which the material is covered, enabling something approaching true self-paced learning. This has helped to bring CAL back into the education (as opposed to training) sector, and UK universities are currently putting a considerable amount of effort into the development of up-to-date CAL systems, under the auspices of the Universities Funding Council's Teaching and Learning Technology Programme (TLTP).

Further developments offer the possibility of 'intelligent' CAL, where the system is able to modify its teaching strategy to suit the individual who is using the system. Not surprisingly, this involves the use of techniques from artificial intelligence. Being able to modify the teaching strategy implies three things about the system:

● It must be able to model the pattern of the student's responses (and therefore presumed knowledge) in some way.

● It must be able to reason about the knowledge it has regarding the subject it is trying to 'teach'. (The 'knowledge' in a conventional CAL system is stored in such a way as to make this impossible.)

● It must allow for flexibility in the interaction between the student and the system.

Some of the current TLTP projects are aiming to deliver intelligent CAL systems; you may find yourself using one while you are at university!

3.14 Business games

The use of management games and simulations for training purposes is one of many ideas which have found their way into business management from a military context; originally it stemmed from the logical extension of military operational 'manoeuvres' to focus on management aspects such as logistics. In a computer-based business game, the business which is being 'managed' is represented as a model in the computer. The model will cover finance, sales, production (it is almost always a manufacturing company, because this is easier to simulate on a computer), the economic environment and so on.

There are essentially two types of business game, the *competitive* and the *open-ended*. In the competitive type, several teams begin with effectively identical simulated companies, and the game proceeds through several rounds of decisions. Each set of decisions typically covers a month or a year in game time, and normally involves exclusively the quantitative aspects of decisions such as prices, staffing levels and investment. Each team must produce its decisions by the deadline for that period, perhaps on a paper decision-form, or increasingly these days by entering the decisions into the computer themselves. The crucial point about the competitive type of game is that the decisions of the different companies interact with each other. So, for example, one team may decide to invest heavily in advertising in the hope of achieving a substantial increase in its market share, but whether or not it will achieve this will depend on what the other teams have decided to do. In this type of business game, the computer model does all of the work in calculating the consequences of the teams' decisions, and the rôle of the umpire is usually limited to changing the parameters which represent the economic environment. There is usually a clear-cut built-in criterion for judging the winner, such as profit or share price. Once developed, these games are very easy to run, and can be bought ready-made from several companies. As well as being common on management training courses, these competitive business games are often run by businesses or newspapers for companies, schools or universities to enter, mainly as a publicity exercise. One problem in educational terms is that this type of game can degenerate into a 'guess how the model works' exercise rather than anything resembling managing a real company. A relatively recent development for the school/university environment is to have other exercises associated with the game whose success affects the company's performance, enabling other techniques to be incorporated. For example, a team's success in an exercise in project management techniques involving the replacement of some of the simulated company's machines over a weekend will determine what levels of production it is possible for the team to achieve next period.

By contrast, the open-ended game is not directly competitive, and indeed may involve only a single team. Here the quantitative model plays only a part in determining the outcomes of the team's decisions. The umpire also adjusts the results to reflect the team's performance on more qualitative aspects. These may range from specific tasks or exercises of the type described above, to a complete simulated electronic mail system allowing the 'managers' in the team open-ended communication with anyone else in their 'world' (workforce, suppliers, customers) as in the ProNet Business game developed at Manchester

Business School. ProNet offers not only a simulated manufacturing company, but also one involving an NHS Trust hospital. Open-ended games offer a much 'richer' learning environment for the players, but require correspondingly more effort from the umpires; there is thus less of a market for off-the-shelf games than with the competitive type.

3.15 Computer games

For many people, especially younger teenagers, computers are synonymous with games. Computers have been used for various kinds of games ever since their invention. Originally, these were games where the speed of interaction was not important, so that they could be played on batch processing systems or systems where the interaction was slow and/or difficult: these included games such as chess, draughts, and various 'mathematical recreations' like John Conway's 'Life' game. In the interactive era this extended into text-based fantasy games of the 'Dungeons and Dragons' type, but it was not until the microcomputer era made home computers really feasible that the highly interactive, graphics-based games came into being. Progress since then has occurred at a remarkable rate, but detailing the history of it is beyond the scope of this book.

Computer games now represent a large market in themselves (so large that it now has spin-offs in the form of records, movies and so on), and one which is now diverging somewhat from the rest of the home computer market, let alone the business computer one with which we are concerned here. The arcade games machines have been joined by special-purpose home computers such as those made by Sega and Nintendo, which cannot be used for anything other than games (see our comments about multi-purpose machines in the Introduction). There does continue to be a games market on more general-purpose home computers as well, but as many of these computers are not IBM compatible, the games market and the business market have few points of commonality, except in the limited area of programming in languages like BASIC or C. Despite these 'divisions', it is worth observing that more mainstream designers could nevertheless learn a lot from the high standard of the human interface on the games machines, especially the colour graphics output displays and the inputs designed for high-speed interaction. Games software and hardware are considerably superior to business systems in these respects, and probably only equalled by one or two military systems, such as those for fly-by-wire aircraft.

It is perhaps not surprising that games are the first commercial applications of the new human interface technologies known as *virtual reality*. These technologies include a helmet which (for output) presents separate pictures to each eye, giving a three-dimensional effect so that the user appears to be in the projected image, and (for input) registers which direction the user is looking and moving in, so that the user can apparently move around in the virtual reality world by moving (in an empty room) in the real world. Another input device is the data glove, which transmits hand and finger movements to the computer, so that the user can also manipulate the objects in the virtual world (for example, pick things up, open doors and so on). No doubt these devices will soon find more business-oriented application; they could just be the face of computing in the 21st century!

3.16 Artificial intelligence

Artificial intelligence (AI) has been an area of active research for over 40 years, with the central theme being the possibility of producing machines which think. At one time, in the immediate post-World War II years, there was little 'distance' between AI research and the work on the first electronic stored-program computers. Indeed, it seemed possible that 'thinking machines' were only a few years away. For example, the mathematician Alan Turing was involved in both the development of the Manchester Mark I computer (see the Introduction) and in the question of how to judge the intelligence of a machine. His speculations on the latter led to what is now called the Turing test. In such a test, a person interacts with a terminal, which is connected either to a machine or to a terminal operated by another human being. If the person cannot distinguish interactions with the machine from those with another human, then the machine may be regarded as intelligent.

During the late 1950s and early 1960s, AI research increasingly diverged from the number-crunching and data processing applications which made up the mainstream of computing. The main emphasis in AI during this period was on systems which possessed some degree of general intelligence or problem-solving ability. This led to such spin-offs as the development of the computer language LISP, which was to become one of the corner-stones of AI research (see section 2.5).

As time went on, although both AI and mainstream computing were concerned with the storage of large amounts of data in one form or another, there was little commonality in the work done. The main concern of mainstream data processing was with structures which permitted the efficient storage and retrieval of data, while AI was more concerned with attempting to produce structures which represented the way in which the human brain stores data/information/knowledge.

Only in the late 1970s did the AI work begin to bear fruit as far as potential mainstream commercial applications were concerned, in the form of rudimentary natural language understanding and of the first expert systems. It took a further 10 years for these developments to come close to being regarded as normal commercial practice. In the meantime, AI research has inevitably progressed still further. Shortly we shall look at some of the areas of AI research which are on the verge of reaching commercial application in business, but first let us make a few remarks about definitions.

Perhaps the most useful definition of AI is that offered by Marvin Minsky: 'AI is the science of making machines do things which would require intelligence if they were done by a human.' We believe that much of the argument over definitions of AI which takes place elsewhere stems from the lack of agreement as to what constitutes *human* (or indeed any other natural) intelligence.

To illustrate this point, computer programs for calculating income tax routinely accomplish tasks which are beyond the abilities (intelligence?) of many humans; microprocessor-based chess computers play chess to a reasonable enough standard to sell in large numbers, if not to a standard which would worry a Grand Master — and some research machines *are* reaching that standard; and conventional computer systems exist which perform tasks such as working out credit ratings, tasks which are often described as requiring human expertise. Indeed, one of the findings of the last 40 or so years of work in AI and other areas of computer science is that there are tasks which humans find difficult which machines can be made to perform well, and conversely tasks which humans find easy which machines at present struggle with.

If you are really worried by it, we would suggest that the use of the adjective intelligent in relation to current commercially feasible computer systems is, at best, extremely misleading — and the source of much unnecessary apprehension.

We shall describe three different areas of AI in this section:

- Natural language understanding

- Pattern recognition

- Speech recognition.

The greatest business success from AI so far, expert systems, has a section to itself (3.11). A brief description of the others follows.

Natural language understanding

The problem of human–computer communication (particularly in the direction from the human to the computer) has existed ever since the computer was invented (see section 2 again!). Ideally, the human should be able to interact with the computer exactly as with another human. As a philosophy, this is virtually identical to the Turing test mentioned above, although ideally we would not wish to restrict the interaction to being via a terminal; this gives some indication of how hard such an ideal might be to attain.

There is still considerable debate about the extent to which computers will ever fully understand sentences in English. Depending on your perspective, English may be seen as either hopelessly imprecise or as permitting the subtlest nuances and shades of meaning. It is true to say that current systems are capable of a degree of natural language *processing*, but not really of any *understanding*. Progress is faster in areas where the natural language is constrained, and especially where it has a substantial proportion of technical terms; thus *intelligent front-ends* to another computer package, such as a database or an operating system, are feasible with current technology.

It is also true that most natural language work has concentrated on the printed word. This is understandable, because the printed word is static and hence easy to replicate for test purposes, and because it avoids the additional problems of having to cope with handwriting or, worse still, speech and voice recognition (see section 10). Thus considerable advances have been made in areas such as machine translation of technical documentation, and automatic abstracting of research reports. Such activities take place routinely in several large corporations, but often still require some human post-translation editing. Most systems cover translation between French and English (in both directions), with either German or Spanish replacing one or other of these being the next most common. Systems including non-European languages are extremely rare, except for Arabic and Japanese; among the most successful machine translation systems for the latter are those produced by Fujitsu (in Japan). However, most of these operate effectively in batch mode on large mainframes, although 'one sentence at a time' translation is now possible. Most existing systems were developed for the corporations concerned, but the sale of machine translation packages is now on the verge of becoming a commercially viable business.

If we consider interactive work, it seems reasonable to argue that speech translation will in the long term be at least as important as translation of the printed word. Unfortunately, speech is not always grammatical, containing errors, interjections, corrections and so on. This means that much of the work on recognizing the printed word does not transfer easily to the spoken word, and so there is a long way to go yet. (See also the sub-section on speech recognition below.)

Pattern recognition

Natural language could be thought of as one form of pattern recognition, but here we mean the far more general activity of visual recognition of patterns, sometimes called *machine vision*. This is extremely important for robotics, and many practical applications now exist. The most common task performed is automated inspection, and the most common users the automobile and electronics industries. It is, however, arguable how much of the credit for these successful implementations belongs to AI, and how much to more conventional signal processing ideas. We shall not pursue this debate here! Despite the successes in robotics for manufacturing, pattern recognition is at present some way away from having direct effects on other business/management problems. It does however seem plausible that successful machine vision would have a considerable effect on security systems such as those for electronic banking which currently work in terms of coded PINs (Personal Identification Numbers). This area is one in which two technological developments offer a lot of potential, namely parallel processing and neural networks; current machine vision has been severely handicapped by the amount of processing power required on a single processor.

Speech recognition

Speech recognition adds another dimension to the problems of natural language understanding. Problems include the effects of background noise, changes in pronunciation according to whether words are spoken in isolation or in a sentence, and variations of accent between individuals. Perhaps the biggest problem of all is that everyday speech is not grammatical, as attempts to transcribe an interview or conversation often reveal. Conversations often include repetitions, corrections and incomplete sentences. Voice recognition goes even further, namely to try to identify the speaker (perhaps for security purposes). Most work given either of the two labels is in fact concerned with *speech* recognition, and this is what we shall deal with in the remainder of this sub-section.

There are two ways in which the problems of speech recognition may be partially eased:

- by restricting the vocabulary of words which may be used

- by restricting the number of users.

Current commercially available systems can only cope with very restricted versions of each of these two cases. For example, the vocabulary may be limited to the digits 0 – 9 and the words 'yes' and 'no' for a so-called *speaker-independent* system, one which will in theory deal with any user. The other possibility is a *speaker-dependent* system, covering a somewhat less limited range of words for a single user, who must 'train' the system to recognize the words as they are pronounced.

Small speaker-independent systems such as the above example, along with non-AI developments such as speech synthesis and digitized recorded speech, form the rapidly developing area of *voicemail* systems for business use, of which Digital's DECVoice is an example. Another use of this technology for speaker-independent systems which has appeared recently is in automated telephone systems such as 'quiz-lines', where multiple-choice answers to the questions limit the range of possible spoken responses.

A particular impetus for improved speech recognition systems in recent years has come from efforts to produce truly pocket-size computers. Machines are already available which are much smaller than a standard keyboard, and many managers are either unable or unwilling to type accurately (electronic mail systems do not yet seem to be replacing the telephone, even if they complement it in useful ways!). Pen-based input is currently the favoured method, but speech input would be a strong contender. Speaker-independent systems with large enough vocabularies to instruct a computer usefully are just becoming available, although at the time of writing they require you to speak with an American accent!

3.17 Multimedia and hypertext

The main forms of output from a computer have always been effectively similar to what is possible in an ordinary book. First there was text: characters on a printer (or a punched card or paper tape), and later on a VDU screen. Along with the VDU screen came graphics; at first little better than could be achieved by printing characters on a printer, but gradually improving over the years, and becoming multi-coloured rather than monochrome, although remaining still rather than moving.

Sound had been technologically possible as an output medium from the earliest days of computing, but had found little commercial use, except for terminals emitting a 'bleep' as a warning to the user, for example when an error had occurred, and a small market in systems for visually handicapped users. Sound did not seem to play a major role in business applications. The advent of the personal computer revolutionized the position of sound in two ways. First, the home computer user was much more interested in the possibilities of using sound on a computer (for example as a background to computer games). Second, the low price of personal computers made it possible to dedicate most of the computer's processing power to a sound-based application. Alongside this change came the digital audio revolution, which made it possible for the first time to record sound using the same techniques as for normal computer data. This in turn led to a revolution in synthesizer technology in music, including the MIDI interface which (amongst other things) enabled a computer, suitably programmed, to play a musical instrument.

Thus a demand now existed for personal computers with good sound reproduction qualities, as well as the ever-improving picture quality. The multimedia revolution was born. As well as sound, the other major step forward was the inclusion of moving pictures, rather than just still ones. At first these were simple, cartoon-style animations, but now it is possible to include video images, although storing a video image does take up a considerable amount of memory. The better-quality screens also mean that it is now possible to display still photographs at a comparable level of quality to the originals.

Naturally it is not enough just for it to be technologically possible to use sound, animated graphics, photographs and moving video as well as text; there also needs to be software to enable systems to be written to do it. There are several specialized markets, including the computer games market, which led the way in terms of sound and motion video, and many aspects of the entertainment industry, where the ability to manipulate sounds and images with a computer is having a considerable influence on music, art, TV and film. Examples range from the ubiquitous sampling keyboard in music to the Rover television commercials which merge 70-year-old film of Buster Keaton into a modern video to show him 'driving' a Rover Metro. The most general potential application of multi-media systems (so far, at least!) is in education and training, to produce something much more exciting than a mere book; unfortunately, we can't do justice to it here, for obvious reasons. The best-known general purpose multi-media software packages are therefore those such as Authorware Professional, which are intended for creating multi-media computer-aided learning systems.

The other major advance which packages such as Authorware Professional incorporate is their use of the hypertext concept, sometimes called hypermedia in this context. Hypertext breaks away from the normal linear structure of any written document such as a book. Rather than the idea that the user/reader should go through from beginning to end, the idea behind hypertext is that the user should be able to dip in and out, browse around, look at the bits which they find interesting, etc. This became possible with the appearance of the graphical user interface (see section 1.2), which makes it possible to point and click on the interesting part. This might be a piece of hot text, where for example the user clicks on a term to see a definition of that term (in a hypertext document that would have happened for graphical user interface in the previous sentence, instead of having to put 'see section 1.2'). Alternatively it might be a button, a small graphic on the screen; click on that, and it will take you to a different place in the document, or run an animation, or whatever is appropriate. Again, this is difficult to show in an ordinary book, but the diary screen shown in Figure 19 in the Personal Diaries section 3.7 is in fact from one of the first hypertext packages, Hypercard. Clicking on the little picture of a house will take you straight to the 'home' screen; clicking on the filing card will take you to the address book and so on.

3.18 Desk-top publishing

Desk-top publishing (DTP) takes the idea of being able to insert output from other packages into what is basically a text-processing package (see section 3.5) one step further. It allows the user to set up blank pages called *templates* of a particular size, shape, number of columns etc., with features such as running headers, logos and so on. This is effectively taking the idea of standard letters mentioned in the word-processing section (3.5) a stage further. Then, virtually *any* text or images which can be produced in the computer may be 'pasted' onto these blank pages to produce anything from a news-sheet to a publicity brochure to an entire book. Indeed, one of the authors has created a book[1] by just such a method — producing all the text with the DTP package Aldus Pagemaker, except for that on the cover. As mentioned in section 3.5, although this was how DTP began, most current word-processing packages are now able to do these things. The success of packages such as Aldus Pagemaker and Quark Xpress has led to complete small businesses springing up to offer a publishing service. All they need is a suitable computer, the DTP software and a laser printer! Note that the reputation of the Apple Macintosh for good graphics has given it a strong presence in the DTP area.

DTP packages continue to evolve, to maintain their lead over ordinary word-processors. Advances include multiple type-styles and sets of fonts within a single page or document, text running vertically or at an angle instead of horizontally across the page, automatic creation of an index or table of contents by 'tagging' the elements which need to be included in it, the ability to exploit colour printers to the full, and so on. One difference between DTP and word-processing packages which is clear when one reads the respective manuals is in the language they use. Much of the vocabulary of DTP has come from the printing/publishing trade, such as kerning (changing the spacing between a pair of letters such as Fi to look better), whereas that of word-processing tends to come from the office environment, and therefore is perhaps more familiar to most people in business.

As with many software advances, although the idea might have been feasible before, it required a hardware advance to make DTP commercially worthwhile. With word-processing, it was the full-screen editing of the VDU; in the case of DTP, it was the laser printer (see section 12.2), which enables its owner to produce (almost) typeset quality documents. Again, technology converges, so that the actual typesetting by publishers and printers is now done using the 'big brother' of PC-based DTP computer systems.

Reference
1. J. S. Edwards *Building Knowledge-based Systems: towards a methodology,* Pitman, London, 1991.

3.19 Computer-aided design

Graphics in general have been mentioned in a separate section (3.4), their intention being to make an impression or convey an idea. The aims of computer-aided design (CAD) are rather different. While still used for conveying ideas and supporting creativity, the critical requirements for CAD are to facilitate precision and visualization. The typical user of a CAD package is therefore an engineer or an architect rather than a sales or marketing person. Before CAD systems were developed, a great deal of time was spent making drawings of the product, bridge or building. These drawings were difficult and time-consuming to modify, and two-dimensional ('flat'). This meant that much of the visualization process which is a necessary part of design had to be carried out inside the designer's head, making it hard to discuss the designs with other people.

CAD packages take us as close as we come in this book to the realms of mathematical computing. The systems not only enable the designer to work with the design interactively, manipulating it in a way which is simply not possible with pen or pencil and paper, but also permit solid objects to be shown in three dimensions (reproduced by perspective on the flat two-dimensional screen of the VDU). Such objects may then be rotated, to allow views from different angles, scaled up or down, and so on. These seemingly simple feats actually take a great deal of computer processing power.

Originally, in the 1970s, the technology required for this graphical manipulation meant that a special-purpose workstation, such as those made by Sun or Apollo, had to be used, effectively delivering the power of a mini-computer to a single user. However, the continuing improvements in technology mean that it is now perfectly feasible to carry out CAD work on a high-specification personal computer, using a package such as AutoCAD. The original workstation-based systems tended to use special graphics pads for inputs such as shape selection, whereas newer systems on both PCs and workstations have graphical user interfaces (see section 1.2) which enable this all to be done on-screen.

In manufacturing engineering, CAD is often extended into CAM (computer-aided manufacture), whereby the computer-based 'drawings' which are the specifications of (say) the parts required, are used directly to control the machines which manufacture them. This is no easy task, since most parts require several different operations to be carried out on several different machines, and it is usually inefficient to reserve a machine exclusively for one type of part. Thus the CAM system must ensure that the combinations of numerically-controlled machine tools carry out the required operations on the right parts and in the correct sequence. At its best, an integrated CAD/CAM system will help to ensure that the requirements of the production process are also taken into account in the design process.

3.20 Statistical analysis and forecasting

As we saw in the Introduction, automating the analysis of census results was one of the key steps on the road which led to the computer as we know it. Today there is a far greater amount of information available from censuses, questionnaires and surveys which needs to be analyzed. Almost every central and local government department, and almost every organization whose customers are the general public, needs access to the results of statistical analyses of large amounts of data; not to mention the large numbers of researchers in universities with similar needs. The analysis required can range from, at the simplest, the straightforward counting tasks for which censuses were originally devised ('how many adults are there in our area who will pay the new Council Tax?'), through calculations of averages and proportions ('how many packets of our brand of tea does each customer buy in a year?', 'what proportion of households in this city own a dishwasher?') to the home territory of statistics ('is our product significantly less reliable than our competitors'?', 'is there an association between how much people eat of this substance and their chance of developing cancer?').

As a result of this large demand for statistical analysis, there is a correspondingly large market for applications packages which carry it out. The subject of statistical analysis itself is beyond the scope of this book; a suitable reference is Fleming and Nellis[1]. If you don't know any statistics, you may safely skip the rest of this section, but it may be a disadvantage in a career in management! The more general statistical packages will perform all the basic functions of elementary statistics as found in any textbook, including descriptive statistics, significance tests, hypothesis testing, correlation, linear regression, analysis of variance and even more advanced techniques. Well-known general packages include SAS, MINITAB and SPSS (Statistical Package for the Social Sciences). Most spreadsheets nowadays have built-in functions for all the standard statistical techniques, but in general do not offer as good facilities for data entry as the statistical packages. This can be vitally important when there are tens of thousands of observations to be analyzed, as is quite usual.

As well as the general-purpose packages, there are also a considerable number of statistical analysis packages for more specialized markets. For example, MARQUIS, MARKPACK and KWIKSTAT (sic) are specifically aimed at practitioners and students of marketing, to help them analyze market research data. There are also specialized statistical packages for use by the medical profession, in quality control for manufacturing, in oil and mineral exploration, and in agriculture, to name but a few. In most cases, the difference between the specialized package and a more general one is not in the functionality so much as in the human interface; the packages use the jargon of the area concerned, so as to make the statistics seem less intimidating. The downside of this ease of use is that the users of specialized packages particularly may not always realize the limitations of the conclusions which they are drawing from their statistical analyses.

Another way to achieve a specialized market is to concentrate on a sub-set of statistical techniques, rather than a wide range. Forecasting is something that all companies have to attempt if they are to plan for the future. Most forecasts attempt to use past data in order to identify short-, medium- and long-term trends, and use this knowledge to project the current position into the future. It is quantitative forecasting, often called time series analysis, which concerns us here; other types of forecasting are usually too judgemental for computers to be of much assistance at present (but see section 3.11).

Although often (correctly) regarded as a sub-set of statistical analysis, the extensive use of forecasting techniques such as curve fitting (for medium-term forecasts) and exponential smoothing (for short-term forecasts) have formed the basis of a reasonably substantial software market.

Packages such as SPSS and the others named above usually offer separate modules which incorporate many of the forecasting techniques currently available. In addition, although not necessarily the best computational environment for analyzing past data, many spreadsheet *add-ons* for forecasting are available. Those which operate with Lotus 1-2-3 include FORECALC, FORECAST!, FORECAST/DSS and Lotus-FORMAN (see Figure 36 in the Appendix 'Spreadsheets (2): macros and menus' for an example of the latter).

Reference
1. M. C. Fleming and J. G. Nellis *The Essence of Statistics for Business,* Prentice Hall, 1991.

3.21 Executive information systems

Executive information systems (EIS) are one of the current 'hot topics' in the information systems world, being a response to the long-standing criticisms of top management, especially in the UK, as failing to reap the benefits of information technology — partly because of being either unwilling or unable to use a standard QWERTY keyboard. Freyenfeld's book[1] discusses this point very well, though it was written before the appearance of the first generation of EIS.

The goal of executive information systems is to provide executive- or director-level support, presumably *decision* support (see section 3.8). This is founded on two principles:

● Question and answer interaction with databases.

● Use of existing databases — proprietary EIS are marketed as add-ons to existing information systems, not rewrites of them or separate stand-alone systems.

Amongst the current market leaders in the UK are:

- Holos from Holistic Systems

- FCS-Pilot from Thorn EMI Computer Software

- Commander from Comshare

The last two are probably the leaders in *world* market share also. Overall, this is a high-powered, and by no means small, market; one EIS installation can cost tens of thousands of pounds in software. Users of Commander include British Steel, while FCS-Pilot's customers include ICI.

There are two basic approaches to the structure of an EIS. One is the downloading of information from the organization's mainframe to the executive's PC, probably on a daily basis. The other is a live PC-mainframe link which allows instantaneous distribution of new data, including external data. One of the features of director-level business decisions is that they are concerned as much with information external to the company, such as market or economic trends, as with internal information. As networking technology has improved, so the 'seamless link' approach has gained ground over the downloading approach, even though senior executives very rarely require 'up to the minute' (as opposed to 'up to last night') data.

Installing an EIS involves a big one-off effort in setting-up the system, to ensure that the mainframe (on which it is assumed that the information is held) transfers data in the right format for the EIS package on the PC to handle. The latest EIS can now cope with information held on the file server of a PC network, where no mainframe as such exists. Most EIS, especially those where the link is always 'live', also include electronic mail facilities in case the organization does not already have them.

A typical approach to information handling and display in an EIS is to convert all downloaded data (wherever it came from) into a standard representation, but then to give considerable flexibility in how the information is retrieved and displayed. This also needs to take into account that the keyboard may not be the preferred input device. Typically, the downloaded database might be a multi-dimensional one with (say) 4 pre-set dimensions:

- Items (profit, cost, etc.)

- Subsidiaries/units

- Actual vs. budget vs. forecast

- Time period.

User input consists of selecting from restricted menus, e.g.

what form of output?

what information?

which part of the company?

There are several hundred pre-defined page formats for tables, graphs, etc., and effectively all the user does is to select the format and the two relevant dimensions of the four to be displayed (e.g. items against time).

A keyboard is thus certainly not *necessary* for input. Devices used instead include:

- Mouse

- Touchscreen

- Special keypad rather like a TV remote control, which only has buttons for the numbers 0 – 9, +, – and a couple of special keys.

Of course, the user *can* use the keyboard if desired!

A special feature of EIS displays is that some of the items on any particular screen are active, so that clicking the mouse or pressing on one of those items sends you down a level of detail. Thus if, for example, total sales are unexpectedly lower than planned, the executive can look at a breakdown of sales by region to see if the problems have a general or specific cause. In EIS circles, this is called a *drill-down* facility, but some people would see this as a use of that other current IT 'hot topic', hypertext (see section 3.17).

Exception reporting is another selling point of EIS. Comshare's Commander was the first to feature 'traffic light'-style exception reporting with 'actual' figures displayed in red, yellow or green colours, according to whether their performance against the 'planned' is unacceptable, dubious or OK.

Reference
1. W. Freyenfeld *Decision Support Systems: an executive overview of interactive computer-assisted decision making in the UK in 1984*, NCC Publications, 1984.

3.22 Simulation

One of the problems faced by business managers and those who seek to assist them, such as operational researchers and management scientists, is that there is no direct management equivalent of the scientist's or engineer's laboratory experiment. This is a pity, because such experiments help in answering one of the key questions implied in any form of planning: 'what will happen if we do this?' Fortunately, such 'what if?' questions can often be examined by the use of a mathematical model, as is mentioned in several places in this book, especially the sections on Spreadsheets. However, there are other types of problem, especially those involving queueing processes or flows, where such an approach is impracticable. This is where computer simulation comes in. To be precise, we should call it Monte Carlo simulation, because to some people (economists for example) anything used for 'what if?' analysis is a simulation, even a mathematical model. Monte Carlo simulation implies the use of random sampling from probability distributions, the name coming from the casino in Monte Carlo and dating back to pre-computer days when roulette wheels were used to generate the random samples (really!).

The way a simulation model works is as follows. Suppose a manager is getting complaints about the queues at a supermarket's check-outs. The manager can't keep changing the number of check-outs which are open in order to see which arrangement works best, and it is impossible to come up with a good mathematical model because there is too much variability in the system. On the one hand, each customer does not take the same length of time to be served: some have only one or two items, others have one or two trolleys-full of goods. Equally, the number of customers arriving is different at different times of the day and week. However, if the manager has data on the distribution of customer arrival times, and on what proportion of customers buy how many items, the operation of a check-out can be simulated by using the computer's random number generation facilities to produce a simulated flow of customers (or a flow of simulated customers, if you prefer to think of it that way) in accordance with the distributions. In the model, check-outs can then be opened or closed, or made into express check-outs ('9 items or fewer only'), just as the manager pleases, to work out what is best for the system without interfering with it in the real world. Similar models can be constructed to simulate many other business systems, especially those involving any kind of movement. Figure 21 shows the output from a stock control simulation, which can be used to test the effect of various different ordering policies.

The latest simulation packages such as WITNESS and STELLA actually allow the manager to 'see' the simulated system operating on the VDU screen (faster than real time), stop it at a point of particular interest, go back to try again with changes to the check-out layout, and so on. Figure 22 shows a screen from a WITNESS simulation of an airport's check-in area.

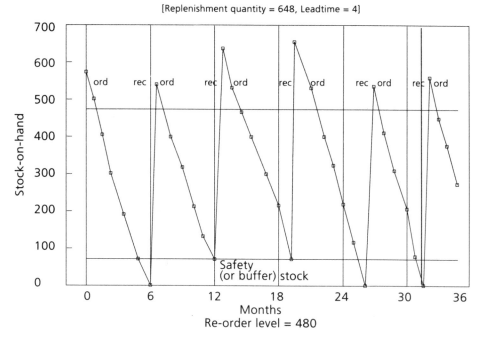

Figure 21 Output from a stock control simulation model

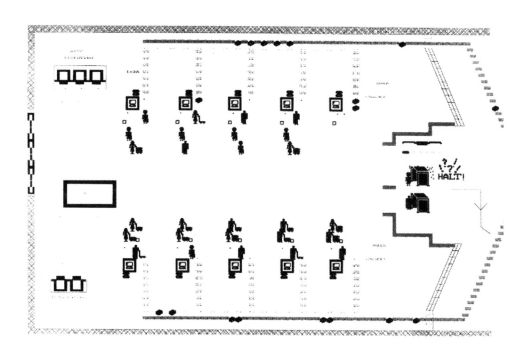

Figure 22 A WITNESS screen showing airport check-in desks

3.23 Computer-aided software engineering

Computer-aided software engineering (CASE) is the term used for software applications packages which help computer systems developers to do their jobs better. The support which these CASE tools offer can cover various aspects of the development, from system design to a project diary. The sections of this book on Systems Development (6 and 7) will tell you that there is a great deal more to it than 'just' programming; systems analysis, design, testing, interaction with the users and so on. On a large project, all of these steps need to be documented, which is a major task in itself. Many decisions have to made during the course of analysis and design, and it is often important for the project team to be able to know who made a particular decision, in case it needs to be reviewed at a later date. CASE tools carry out this function, but also provide more specific support for tasks such as the considerable amount of drawing of diagrams which needs to take place during systems analysis and design. This is much more specific support than general software packages for graphics (see section 3.4) will provide. A CASE tool will, for example, keep lists of the names of the entities which have been included in a diagram or set of diagrams. In fact, one of the few aspects of systems development for which CASE tools do not provide specific support is the actual programming, i.e. the writing of the programs themselves.

In order to provide the support for the developers, some assumptions have to be made about *how* the system is going to be developed. As a result, most CASE tools are linked with a particular method or methodology for systems development (see again sections 6 and 7). For example:

- the CASE tools IEF and IEW support the Information Engineering methodology;

- the CASE tool Excelerator supports the Structured Analysis and Design methodology;

- several CASE tools, including ASSET and SSADM Engineer, support the UK government-backed methodology SSADM.

3.24 Project management

One of many areas in which the advent of personal computers with good graphics has made the manager's life easier is that of project management. The management of a complex project, such as building an office block, replacing a generator in a power station, or designing a large computer system, is a difficult task, partly because such a project consists of a large number of separate but interconnected activities; there could easily be as many as 25,000 of them.

Techniques to help with project management have been available since the 1950s; they include critical path analysis and PERT (Project Evaluation and Review Technique). Critical path and PERT enable the manager to work out the answers to key questions such as: 'what is the minimum time in which we can complete the project?' or 'which activities must we be extra certain to keep to the plan?' These calculations are very valuable, but project management packages can do more. The packages are able to show the activities of the project in the form of various diagrams, for example a form of bar chart called a Gantt chart, or a network diagram. The latter represents logical constraints on the order of the activities in the project, such as the need to lay the foundations of a building before starting to build the walls. Figure 23 shows a simple example of a network diagram, the numbers representing different activities.

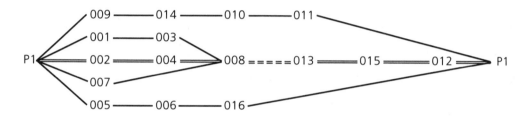

Figure 23 A simple network diagram from a project management package

These views of the project help the manager(s) to understand what is happening, both in planning the project before it starts, and in monitoring and controlling it while it is going on. Indeed, the power of the graphical output is so impressive that in the 1960s, when computers could produce the numerical calculations but not the graphics, companies often found it worthwhile to have their drawing office staff produce the network diagram by hand from the computer print-out — even though this process might take days for a large project!

There is a wide range of packages currently available for project management, from those which are aimed at the '25,000 activity' kind of project, to those intended for more modest projects with 'only' a hundred activities or so. Even running a project of the latter size is still complex enough for an individual manager to need the computer support provided by project management software, particularly in terms of allocating resources (including people) to the various activities. The packages now allow you not only to specify that (say) putting in the door-frames needs to be done by a carpenter, but which carpenter is to do it. Their use has gradually spread from construction and engineering to computing, and now to such diverse fields as organizing a conference, planning an audit visit, and designing and introducing a new product. Project management packages include Artemis, Primavera, PERTMASTER, SuperProject, PMW and Instaplan, to name but a few. Their prices range from under a hundred pounds to several thousand pounds, depending (at least in part!) on the capabilities and facilities they offer.

3.25 Business accounts packages

All businesses require to keep track of their financial interactions with their customers and suppliers and also have the choice of whether to remunerate their employees through an internally run payroll or use that run by an external agency. If businesses buy and sell goods in addition to services, they will also need to maintain stock records.

The various, but essential, business activities indicated above, which most companies today would wish to control using a computer, are based on several recording systems such as:

- Sales ledger — a record of the financial interactions between a company and its customers

- Purchase ledger — a record of the financial interactions between a company and its suppliers

- Nominal (or general) ledger — a record of the transactions and balances between other elements of the accounting system, in particular the sales and purchase ledger

- Payroll — a record of the financial interactions of a company and its employees which, based on information provided by the company, establishes the remuneration due to each employee and whether that remuneration is in the form of bank credit transfers or as traditional 'pay-slips' with cash

- Stock control — a record of the issues and receipts of stocked items — which clearly can interact with both the purchase and sales ledger but which, on its own account, requires to maintain control of stock levels.

Other business features which a company may also require to be available as part of a business accounts software package include:

- Job costing — which is necessary to analyze and control labour costs derived from employee time-sheets

- Stock usage — linked to the stock control system

- Direct purchases — linked to the purchase ledger

- Miscellaneous costs to account for unspecified costs or charges.

  Such a system not only provides a detailed summary of costs to date, but also permits job costing details to be transferred to the invoicing system and modified to suit before the production of the final invoice.

- Invoicing and sales order processing — which integrates with the sales and nominal ledger as well as the stock control system and maintains surveillance of credit control

- Purchase order processing — which also interacts with other ledgers and organizes how and when orders on wholesale, retail and other customers are placed.

Clearly, although strictly a national market because of the different financial regulations currently operating outside the UK, the market for such business accounts software within the UK is substantial. As a result, good packaged 'solutions' aimed at the smaller business have been established over a period of at least a decade. This means that such packages, with a ten year long pedigree, have proven reliability having *ironed out* all the *bugs* (errors) that may have been around originally. The business accounts software market, therefore, is one of packages offering routine business applications with guaranteed transactional accuracy.

The two main software houses producing general-purpose business accounts packages, Sage and Pegasus, claim to have over 80% of the market share with well over 100,000 clients, and like most of their rivals offer annual software maintenance agreements which provide their clients with guaranteed updates to take into account changes in legislation, tax bands, VAT changes, etc. Such software maintenance agreements also offer telephone Help-desk facilities, but only guarantee to re-instate a system which has *crashed,* due to disk failure and the like, if disks are backed up in a specified manner and hard-copy records have been stored correctly (see section 9). Changes in technology are also accommodated such that the most recent business accounts software for personal computers, for instance:

- recognizes the increasing rôle that faxes play in the business world and offers direct faxing facilities rather than the production of hard copy for subsequent copying within a fax machine

- recognizes the increasing use of LANs (Local Area Networks) within business organizations such that access to a system is by individual password and then access to records is denied if that record is currently being updated by another user on the system (this latter feature has had to be provided on mainframe accounts systems ever since multi-user interactive systems were introduced).

Because training is clearly essential for correct and efficient operations of business accounts software packages, most software houses developing this type of material offer extensive training programmes for their client companies.

Although originally all business accounts software packages for PC operation were developed in a command-driven DOS environment, again more recent developments have recognized the increasing use of the graphical user interface Windows environment. This has brought about the development of Windows-based packages which are *upwardly compatible* with their DOS predecessors, i.e. the newer (Windows) version can use all the data from the older (DOS) version without any need for modification or conversion. This is an absolute necessity where vast amounts of active data need to be transferred from the old to the new system.

Most business accounts software packages were originally developed in a twin floppy disk environment, which imposed severe limitations on the size and number of accounts that could be created in addition to the disk space required for the actual programs. For this reason, the packages were originally marketed as collections of separate modules which could be run either in a stand-alone mode or integrated with other modules within a suite.

Today, with the prevalence of hard disk machines, the number of accounts that can be created is more a function of the software design than disk capacity. Because of the improved efficiency that can be gained by using a single, large, relational database (see Appendix 3) at the heart of the system, most of the more recent business accounts packages are only available as complete, integrated systems rather than as a series of stand-alone elements or modules which can be integrated. The exceptions to these general rules are payroll and job costing.

Most business accounts packages operate on an 'open-item' accounts basis whereby transactions are held on file until fully balanced by corresponding credits and debits. Hence, for example, a customer invoice would be held on file until balanced by a corresponding single payment or series of part payments. Only when the invoiced amount and the payment amount matched could the transaction be regarded as *history*, at which stage it would generally be committed to hard copy before being purged from the system to maintain disk capacity and integrity.

Since the principal function of a business accounting system is to highlight exceptions, accounts packages offer standard exception reporting facilities such as:

- Aged debtor reports, i.e. customers in debt to the company or in excess of their credit limit (a facility which can also be linked to the automatic generation of debt-chasing letters)

- Purchase order listings, i.e. lists of stock items that have fallen below their re-order level and which, therefore, need re-ordering

- Sales reports sorted by:

  turnover balance

  salesperson

  sales area

  credit limit, etc.

- Lists of customers by:

  turnover

  balance owing

- List of invoices overdue on a specified date

- Lists of non-active customers

- VAT reports on both sales and purchases

In addition, they should also allow for customized report generation as specified by the user, such that it would be possible to create a special listing of, for example:

- Customers in a certain sales area, with at least a certain turnover with the company, the format of which could be stored for future use if required on a regular basis for promotional purposes, etc.

a) Sales Ledger

The Sales Ledger in any accounting system records the interaction of a company with its customers. In broad terms it can identify:

- when customers placed orders

- whether and when customer orders were fulfilled

- whether and when customers have been invoiced for orders delivered

- whether and when customers have paid their invoices fully or only partially or, if allowed credit, whether the account is within the credit allowance agreed.

Features of a good Sales Ledger would allow for the identification of:

- Best customers listed in descending order, thus establishing the top twenty percent of customers who, typically, generate eighty percent of the company's sales revenue

- Sales history related to time, thus identifying peak sales times, etc.

- Sales history related to territory, thus identifying best sales areas, etc.

b) Purchase Ledger

Similar in operation to the Sales Ledger, the Purchase Ledger maintains records of a company's interactions with its suppliers. A significant feature of any Purchase Ledger would be to allow a company to control its payments to suppliers in-line with overall company policy. In the UK, unlike the rest of Europe, it would appear to be bad business practice to pay debts too quickly; businesses in England and Wales have the worst record in Europe for paying their bills on time, taking over 50 days on average *(The Guardian,* 16 December 1991).

c) Nominal Ledger

The Nominal Ledger holds a series of nominal accounts — specifically nominated by the user — for recording the financial transactions of the company and providing the information for the company's most crucial reports, namely:

- Profit and loss account

- Trial balances

- Balance sheet

- VAT report.

Although the company running the accounting system can specify any set of nominal accounts, these are usually grouped into the following categories:

- Fixed assets (valuation of buildings and plant)

- Current assets (debtors, cash at bank, VAT on purchases)

- Current liabilities (creditors, VAT on sales)

- Long-term liabilities (loans, overdraft etc.)

- Expenditure

- Revenue (i.e. income).

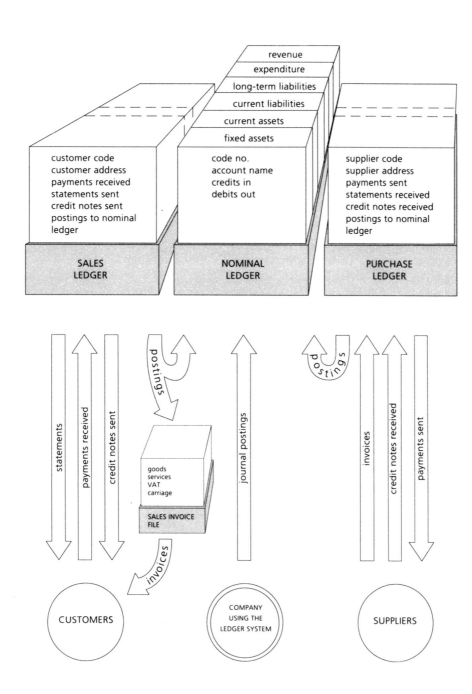

Figure 24 The nominal ledger

The Nominal Ledger is the heart of any accounting system and must be maintained such that reported debits and credits received as *postings* from the sales and purchase ledger always balance out.

A diagrammatic view of the nominal ledger and its interactions with other elements of a complete business system is shown in Figure 24.

d) Stock Control

The Stock Control element of a business accounts package maintains records of the movement of stock items in terms of receipts and withdrawals and interacts with both the purchase ledger (for items ordered by the company and subsequently received into stores) and the sales ledger (for items ordered by customers and withdrawn from stores for onward delivery).

Typical reports generated are:

- Stocktaking lists for verifying the computer systems's figures for quantities of stock held with the reality

- Outstanding order lists for identifying items that have been ordered but not received

- Stock valuation analysis for establishing valuation of stocks held and potential sales valuation

- Stock movement reports, particularly slow movers.

e) Payroll

Although precisely defined, the calculations involved in establishing employees' earnings and resulting payments to be made after tax, national insurance, pension deductions, etc. are relatively complicated and thus tedious to calculate manually. Companies with as few as half-a-dozen employees have therefore found it cost effective to maintain a computerized payroll system.

Because of the regular changes that occur in payroll calculations due to changes in regulations, changes in tax bands, etc. all payroll packages require to be updated at regular intervals, usually through a maintenance agreement with the originating software house.

Payroll packages have to meet designated standards by establishing specified outputs on trial data and offer a variety of options such as:

- Gross to net calculations via standard deductions established from tables such as for income tax or national insurance

- Printing of pay-slips with payment via cash, cheque or bank giro

- A break-down of the number of each denomination of notes and coins needed to make up exactly the correct amount of wages for each individual paid in cash

- End-of-year procedures for producing the details for official forms such as P45, P11 and P14/P60.

Conclusion

Because virtually all businesses now control their finances using computers, the business accounts package market is large and well supplied by a variety of software houses. Because the market is well established, the leading software houses offer a variety of different, well proven general-purpose systems aimed at client companies usually on a size basis and number of accounts to be held. Competitor software houses tend to specialize with products aimed at a specific market sector for whom the general-purpose package might not be appropriate, a good example of the latter being specialized packages developed for General Practitioner (doctor) practices which as well as dealing with finance tend to place far more emphasis on the recording of patient information. Larger companies may well still need to have a system written to order, rather than relying on a proprietary package, however.

3.26 Personnel records systems

While the various business accounting systems keep track of one of the vital assets of a company, its capital, personnel records systems help to keep track of another – the people the company employs. Indeed, in service organizations, the employees themselves may represent the company's principal asset. You may be surprised to find that payroll systems (the ones which calculate wages and salaries) and personnel systems are often completely separate. The reasons for this are mainly historical, in that typically the systems were used by different parts of the company. Payroll (which might even have been called Wages) was clearly part of accounts, whereas personnel clearly was not. Only in the last ten years or so have the advantages of combining these two systems been realized.

A further factor in this was that in the early days of business computing, personnel and computing professionals tended to regard each other with a certain amount of mutual suspicion. This was because both sides felt that personnel records were not really 'computing' in the sense of calculation, but more a question of information storage and retrieval. As a result, the first computer-based personnel records systems were often a 'leap in the dark' for both parties, being the first venture into database systems. These problems have long since disappeared as personnel systems have become more widespread.

Name:		Initials:	Title:		First Name:
Thompson		I R	Mr		Ian

Date of birth:	Date of joining:	Date of leaving:
07/12/67	04/09/89	

Sex:	Marital Status:	Children:	Nationality:
M	Married	1	British

Current Post:	Department:	Location:
Project Leader	Information Systems	Head Office

Previous Posts:

Systems Analyst	Information Systems	Head Office

Current Salary:	Previous Salary:	Date of increase:
£23500	£22600	01/09/93

Company Pension Scheme:	Method of Payment:
Yes	BACS

Last Performance Appraisal:	Appraiser:	Result:
20/07/93	R Hill	4

Home Address:	Telephone:
99 Madeup Street, Anytown, AN1 2DU	011-246 9876

Next of Kin:

Mrs Pamela Thompson (wife)

Address and telephone as above

Highest Educational Qualification:	Subject:
Honours degree	Business Studies

A levels:	O levels/GCSE:	Languages:
4	8	French, German

Other remarks:

Qualified First Aider

Secretary Company Cricket Team

Figure 25 Part of an employee's personnel record

Modern personnel records systems contain not only basic data such as an employee's name, address, date of birth and job title. In addition, the system will contain a history file, showing all the jobs that person has held in the organization, together with dates of promotions, transfers and pay increases. The system will also have detailed individual information: educational qualifications, next of kin, language skills, training courses attended, perhaps also performance appraisal information. Thus the system can be used to handle enquiries such as finding all the sales staff who can speak Spanish, or what proportion of the shopfloor workforce has first aid training. Figure 25 shows an example of what part of an employee's personnel record might look like.

3.27 Process control

Another vital use of computers, principally in manufacturing companies, is for process control. A modern factory (or manufacturing facility, as it is perhaps more likely to be termed), whether a production line or a blast furnace, is extremely complex, with probably a high degree of automation. Controlling it effectively requires large amounts of data to be collected and monitored, and rapid responses put into action when necessary. Both of these tasks may be assisted by computers, which can be linked directly to the factory's equipment, so that data is collected and input to the process control computer system 'on-line' and in real time. Note that what we are talking about here is more than just isolated 'robots' doing particular operations on the production line, though this is also an important application of computing technology. In process control, for example producing chocolates at firms such as Cadbury's, Rowntree's or Terry's, the computer system monitors and controls the speed at which the line moves (perhaps stopping it automatically if there is a problem), checks the temperature of the chocolate, and so on. Process control systems have even been linked to expert systems (see section 3.11) which, when a problem occurs, advise the human operators on what is wrong and what to do about it. One of the best examples of such an expert system is LINKMAN, originally designed for the control of the cement kilns at Blue Circle Cement.

3.28 Geographical information systems

Storing a map inside a computer and retrieving it in a useful form are difficult tasks compared with adding up the items on an invoice or retrieving personnel information. They require hardware which can:

● store large amounts of information (a map the size of an A4 page requires about 1000 times the storage space of a page of words stored as characters)

- retrieve it quickly

- display it (preferably in colour)

- allow it to be manipulated using the mouse or a similar input device.

Only since the mid-1980s has computing technology been up to this challenge on workstations or personal computers rather than mainframe systems, but developments in this field have quickly given rise to the area now known as Geographical Information Systems or GIS. Obviously such systems were always going to be of considerable interest to map-makers like the Ordnance Survey, since it is much easier to update a map which is stored in machine-readable form in a computer than to alter the printed version. However, GISs also have many other uses. Local authorities have begun to produce GISs showing where the mains services (electricity cables, water pipes, etc.) are, to try to avoid the problems which arise when, for example, a road repair crew punctures a water main because they didn't know it was there. They also use GISs for activities such as planning new roads and preserving natural habitats. British Gas has spent three years transferring all of its gas pipe route information from paper maps into its GIS. Retail companies such as Tesco[1] use GISs which combine maps with population and consumer survey information from a conventional database to help plan the location of new retail outlets, especially the out-of-town superstores, and distribution warehouses. Oil and mining companies use GISs to store geological information and identify possible new exploration sites. The Royal Institute of Chartered Surveyors has recently demonstrated a pilot version of a system called Domesday 2000; a GIS intended to integrate the many databases around the UK holding information on the use, ownership and value of land. This would be of use to a wide range of people and organizations, from property developers to house- buyers, and from farmers to City firms looking to re-locate out of London. Such information is currently held by a wide range of groups, including the Land Registry, the Ordnance Survey, the Valuation Office, the Department of the Environment, local councils and firms of surveyors. Technologically, the integration of all this information into a networked computer system is perfectly feasible, but its development will depend on whether there is the will to co-operate, especially from the government departments.

Like all special-purpose systems, GISs are quite expensive — the cost of software and hardware for a personal computer-based system is likely to be £10,000 or more, while a workstation-based system might cost three times that figure. However, there is one aspect of GIS which has found a mass market. Route-finding packages, both for companies and individuals, are available which advise you on the best way to get from A to B by road. PC versions of these packages, such as Autoroute Plus and Milemaster 2, can now be bought for only a few hundred pounds. These systems not only give shortest routes, but can also give quickest routes (which may be different), routes avoiding major cities, routes with prescribed stopping points, and so on.Whatever the type of GIS, the European Community's moves towards a single market are sure to mean that the geographical base of many systems will have to expand to cover the whole of Western Europe, not just the UK; some of the route-finding packages already do this.

Reference
1. Stuart Moore and Glen Attewell 'To be and where not to be: the Tesco approach to locational analysis', *OR Insight,* Vol. 4, No.1, pp.21–24, 1991.

3.29 Mailing lists

The use of computer databases of suitably-categorized names and addresses has formed the basis of a whole new line of business, the direct mail industry. Direct mail companies endeavour (with a greater or lesser degree of sophistication) to build up databases based on consumer spending profiles. This, when done well, enables potential customers to receive promotional material which is specifically relevant to them. When used in conjunction with word-processing systems, the letters sent out may not only be *personalized* (i.e. the recipient's name and address put in in a style that matches the rest of the letter, so that you 'can't see the join'), but also *tailored,* so that the text of the offer or advertisement itself is changed slightly according to the specific profile of the recipient. When combined with sophisticated database searches, this can be a very effective tool. For example, a bank may wish to advertise the new 'through the wall' banking facilities at a certain branch. By doing a postcode search to draw up the mailing list, individual letters announcing the new development may be sent not only to customers with accounts at that branch, but also to those with accounts at other branches of the same bank who live in the area. As another example, an insurance company may send out a special offer on car insurance rates to teachers and nurses, having identified the teachers and nurses amongst its existing customers for other types of policy by picking up the 'Occupation' field on its database.

The particular types of selective mailing which we have set out here are what may be termed 'good' use of mailing lists. You may already be aware from examples reported in the newspapers and on television that there are also examples of very 'bad' mailing systems. For example, companies get hold of a list of names and addresses (possibly by dubious means) and send all the material they have to everyone on the list — the 'junk mail' industry rather than true direct mail! This kind of 'blunderbuss' or 'scatter gun' approach goes against all the principles of good marketing, and gets the whole of the direct mail industry a bad name. As a result, national governments and the European Community are seeking to introduce more stringent legislation to regulate the collection and use of mailing list data, although there is controversy over the latest EC proposals at the time of writing, which many feel go too far. In particular, the objectors believe that the copyright in the contents of databases will not be sufficiently protected to make the effort of compiling a good one worthwhile.

Part D
THE MANAGEMENT OF BUSINESS COMPUTING

This and the succeeding sections look at the issues involved in managing computing and information technology in business. The average organization will have many computer users, perhaps in diverse geographical locations, certainly not all in one office! Some users, especially those 'on the road' such as the sales force or auditors, will require machines which are portable. Others may need machines which are capable of functioning in adverse operating conditions, for example extremes of heat (steel industry) and cold (oil and gas exploration), out of doors (surveyors) or in hazardous environments (chemical plants). No one system will meet the needs of the whole business: even the smallest organization these days may well need accounts, database and word-processing facilities. A company may therefore have hundreds of different computer systems.

The managers responsible for business computing — which nowadays includes just about every manager in the organization — must acquire the necessary hardware and software, which may involve employing staff to develop, maintain and operate systems. They must make sure that the systems fit the people who are to use them, and the tasks they need to carry out. They must also ensure that these systems are available for use when needed, but not for use by unauthorized people or for unsanctioned purposes. Finally, this must all be done in such a way that the organization achieves value for money from its investment or, better still, a competitive advantage.

The following sections look at different facets of this responsibility: money, organizational aspects, system development, people and security.

4 | Money

Computing and information technology now forms an extremely large sector of the economies of developed countries. It is not simply a question of organizations spending money on buying new hardware and software, although this element is substantial. There are many other categories of expenditure on computing, including:

- maintaining existing systems

- connecting equipment together

- buying consumables (disks, paper, printer ribbons, etc.)

- advice from consultants

and last (but greatest rather than least)

- paying their own computing staff.

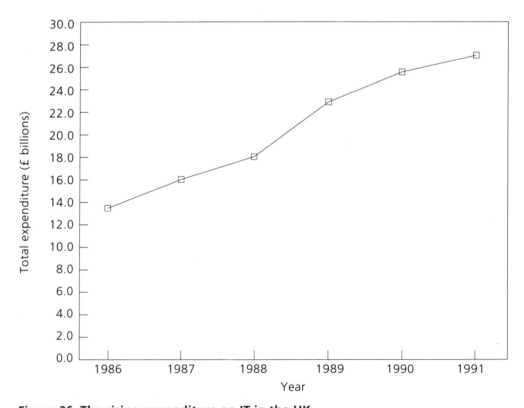

Figure 26 The rising expenditure on IT in the UK

Table 9 shows a breakdown of this expenditure in the UK in 1991, while Figure 26 shows how the total expenditure almost exactly doubled in a period of 5 years.

Table 9 IT expenditure in the UK (OTR-Pedder/CUYB survey for 1991)

Total expenditure 1991	£27.1 Bn
Made up of:	
Hardware	£5.45 Bn
Software and services	£5.13 Bn
Supplies	£0.75 Bn
Communications services	£0.61 Bn
Internal computing staff	£7.38 Bn
Hardware breaks down:	
Micros	£1.66 Bn
Small minis (≤15 users)	£0.72 Bn
Medium minis (16-128)	£0.78 Bn
Large mainframes (>128)	£1.91 Bn
Communications hardware	£0.38 Bn
Software and services includes:	
Hardware maintenance	£1.56 Bn
Contract programming	£0.84 Bn
Software maintenance	£0.73 Bn
Packaged applications	£0.51 Bn
Packaged systems/utilities	£0.49 Bn
IT consultancy	£0.37 Bn

As you can see from the table, UK business and government together spend over £500 per year on computing equipment for every man, woman and child in the country!

The amount spent, not surprisingly, varies considerably between different sectors of the economy. Precise figures on this expenditure are hard to come by. Table 10 shows the expenditure for 1988, which gives a good idea of the amount of variation involved, and also of the high-spending and low-spending areas. Remember there were special factors at work in that period, affecting the two highest-spending areas in particular. The figure for financial institutions was increased by de-regulation, which removed some of the barriers between different sectors of the finance business; a lot was therefore spent on new systems for the new businesses. The figure for the energy and water industry, on the other hand, was affected by the impending privatization; a rush to acquire computer systems and equipment before there were shareholders to worry about the effect this was having on their profits. Note however that these sectors would almost certainly be amongst the highest spenders in any case; as we said earlier in the book, many financial institutions would not be able to do any business without their computer systems. To give you some idea of the scale of computer operations involved in the finance industry, let's look at one of them at around the same period to which those figures apply, Barclays Bank plc.

As at the end of 1988, Barclays Bank had more than 1100 systems staff. They were responsible for 169 separate systems. 16 of these were new in 1988, and some 20 more were planned for development by the end of 1989. One of the largest of these was the book-keeping system which keeps track of all the customer accounts. It comprised some 4000 separate programs, and had interfaces to 25 other systems. Barclays had decided to re-write this system because of all the recent changes in the banking business such as interest-bearing current accounts; they estimated that this would require 500 person-years of development effort.

Table 10 Expenditure per employee by industry sector 1988

Top three were:		
	Financial institutions	£4847
	Energy/water	£2564
	Local government	£1219
	AVERAGE	£840
Typical low values were:		
	Construction	£263
	Health	£200

At present there is a great debate (you might even call it an argument) about the economic merits of moving from mainframe systems to networks of personal computers; *downsizing,* as it is called. No-one disputes that it now appears to be cheaper in the long run to buy personal computers than a mainframe to serve the equivalent number of users, nor that there are some costs involved in supporting departmental computing. The key question is, how large are the hidden costs; items such as the time that the 'departmental computer wizard' spends helping his or her colleagues instead of doing his or her own work? Butler Cox priced a 128-user system on a mini-computer and a PC network, and the 5-year cost of the PC network came out 12% cheaper — £615,000 as against £695,000. This was because the annual recurrent costs for the mini-computer system were twice as much as for the PCs. However, this excluded the costs of staff and applications development. A more recent survey into the cost of personal computer ownership by KPMG Management Consulting (*PC Week,* April 20th 1993) found that 91% of the costs of running a personal computer in a business were hidden costs. The major component of these was the time spent by the unofficial PC experts in the user departments solving everyone else's PC problems. Their figures for total running cost were £5914 per user per year, excluding networking costs. Research by organizations such as the Gartner Group and Forrester Research agree that these hidden costs may be more than a thousand pounds per PC user per year, even if they do not come as high as KPMG's estimates! Figures from Xephon (*Computing,* 15 April 1993), which also attempt to account for these hidden support costs, therefore come to a very different conclusion from that of Butler Cox. Over 5 years, they estimate that the cost of mini- and mainframe systems per user ranges from £4680 to £5973, depending on the precise hardware and software used, whereas that of a network of personal computers ranges from £9400 to £15,000, more than twice as much.

Problems such as an end-user phoning the organization's help desk and saying 'my hard disk is full' just did not arise in pre-personal computer days. The only real solution is for someone to sit down at the machine alongside the end-user so that they can work out together which files may safely be deleted. This takes up the time of both of the people involved.

You will see that these hidden costs can make a big difference to the cost equation. However, partly because of the very nature of *hidden* costs, and also partly because of the vested interests of different manufacturers involved, this debate is far from being resolved at present; and of course the balance of costs changes from year to year as technology progresses.

5 | Organizational aspects

All changes to organizational systems should be evaluated. Computer systems particularly need evaluation, as they often represent a drastic change in working practice, one with a substantial initial capital outlay, and a redirection of expenditure from labour to equipment.

In this section we shall consider the problems of performance measurement for (or 'measuring the success of') computer systems. This will also raise issues of looking at the performance of the business system whose operation the computer system is intended to support. Looking out from the computer system to the organizational system is a 'hot topic' in management circles at the moment, under the title of *business process re-engineering*. What this does *not* mean is 'changing the problem so that the solution fits it'! Rather, it is a recognition that if you simply computerize a business process which is not doing the right things anyway, then all you achieve is to do the wrong things faster, or with fewer mistakes. This is a larger-scale version of the old computing adage: 'Garbage In, Garbage Out'. It therefore makes sense to look at the business aspects of any new development rather than just the computing ones.

There has recently been a series of disastrous attempts to implement computer systems which have been well-publicized in the national press. These include:

- The Stock Exchange's TAURUS system for automated settlement of share dealings cost the Stock Exchange £75 million over four years, and brokers and others far more than this amount, but was never implemented at all.

- The London Ambulance Service's £1.5 million vehicle despatch control system came to a complete standstill when extended to cover the whole of the London area, and may have to be completely scrapped.

- The Performing Rights Society (which collects and distributes royalty payments on recorded music) is being sued by a group of artistes led by the rock band U2 after spending £11 million pounds on a new on-line computer system; the system was never implemented and some £8 million appears to have been wasted.

- Unnecessary expenditure on computer systems by Wessex Regional Health Authority to the tune of tens of millions of pounds, led to the resignation of some of their most senior executives.

We do not claim to know all the answers to avoiding problems such as these (we could make a very good living as consultants if we did!), but all of them centre as much on business aspects as technological ones. Certainly in both the

Stock Exchange and London Ambulance Service, the difficulties were more to do with people failing to agree on what was needed (but one party carrying on anyway), or making promises which they knew could not be kept, rather than anything to do with the technology. Please remember that most computer systems *do* work — but a system which works properly isn't 'news'!

Why measure performance?

We have already stated that all changes of any kind to organizational systems should be monitored, so that their success (or otherwise) may be measured. Indeed, monitoring of all activities is, or at least should be, a key element of managing the organization (see, for example, Humble[1]).

Nevertheless, many managers, whether their responsibilities lie in computer systems or elsewhere, seem to be content with 'getting the change working' without ever sitting down afterwards and looking at precisely what the new system has achieved. In particular, the transition from a manual to a computer system (or from an existing computer system to a new one) is often so disruptive and chaotic that short-term considerations, such as simply ensuring that the new system discharges its basic functions at all, override everything else.

Why, then, are we interested in measuring the success of a new system? There are three principal reasons:

(i) to monitor the extent to which the system meets its predicted performance objectives;

(ii) as justification for the actions which were taken;

(iii) to enable the organization to learn from what happened.

In the complex, rapidly-changing business world of today, it is almost inevitable that any action will have slightly different consequences from those originally intended. The more far-reaching the changes, the harder they will be to predict precisely. It is therefore essential to carry out explicit monitoring of a new system, rather than relying on *ad hoc* or informal feedback on its performance.

Justification should not be seen here purely in the narrow sense of 'guarding your back', or as a paper exercise in creative accounting. Whatever type of organization they run, the managers are responsible for the way in which they run it. Whether this responsibility is to the shareholders of a limited company, to the local population served by a local government department, or to each other as the firm's co-owners, the managers should be in a position to justify the time, effort and money spent on organizational changes.

Most managers would admit the need for monitoring and justification, albeit sometimes rather grudgingly, but organizational learning is often completely forgotten. This may be because it doesn't show directly on the balance sheet! However, it is at least as important for the long-term viability of the organization.

Three components of the organizational learning are worth distinguishing here:

(i) lessons about the particular system being changed;

(ii) lessons about the type of 'solution' which was tried;

(iii) improved skills and expertise on the part of those involved with the change.

Example: a company wishes to improve its system for taking customers' orders. In the old paper-based system, all orders are processed on the basis of written information, either from the customer or taken down over the telephone in a somewhat haphazard manner. The new computer system, based on interactive use of VDUs by telephone staff, allows all orders to be phoned in. For such a change, specific benefits under the three headings mentioned above might include:

● a better understanding of how customers' orders are distributed across different times of day and different days of the week

● practical knowledge of how the response time of the computer used varies with the number of simultaneous users

● more expertise in database work in the data processing department, job enrichment for the order processing clerks (who now speak directly to customers), more knowledge of telecommunications from setting up the answering system.

Bearing in mind all the considerations we have just outlined, it is clear that measuring the success of a new system is a very broad concept, which can only be done in relation to a particular organization and its needs.

Unfortunately, when the change involves a computer system, this concept has often been confused with the narrower issue of whether or not the system meets its specification. One historical reason for this was the traditional insularity of data processing departments, leading to exactly the 'guarding your back' style of justification mentioned earlier. ('We've built the system we think you asked for, so stop complaining.') Whilst it is important to be able to assess the performance of a system in this sense, it is not enough for a business system, since the specification is itself only an interpretation of the original business need.

We will therefore distinguish three levels of measuring the success of a system: evaluation, validation and verification (see Figure 27). Unfortunately, some people use the terms validation and verification the other way round; we had to pick one or the other for use here.

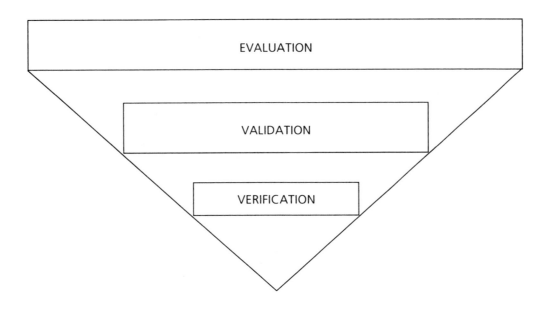

Figure 27 Three levels of measuring the success of a system

Evaluation is the highest-level concept, and thus the broadest. It's the one which we have been addressing so far — 'has the system contributed towards the organization's overall success?'

Validation is part of evaluation, though a very important one; O'Keefe et al[2] refer to it as 'the cornerstone of evaluation'. It is concerned with the performance of the system as constructed, i.e. does the system work acceptably, viewed as a computer system for the task envisaged?

Verification is a narrower concept still, being the term we shall use for assessing whether or not a system meets its specification, irrespective of how that specification was produced or its relevance to the task or to the organization.

It is important to realize that these are three different concepts. Examples abound of systems 'built to spec', i.e. successfully verified, which do not function in practice because crucial elements were omitted from the specification. The systems thus fail at the validation level. Similarly, a system may be perfectly valid, and yet not able to be used properly in the organization, for example because of developments elsewhere, or circumstances not directly connected with the computer system. One of the authors encountered an example where a conventional computer system 'failed' overall because of the lack of a telephone in the office where the terminal was situated; this made it impossible to integrate the system into the normal working routine of the people who were expected to use it.

This distinction between verification and validation is similar to, but not identical to, one which you may have encountered elsewhere: that between efficiency ('doing things right') and effectiveness ('doing the right things'). Thus it is inefficient in terms of cost and space to have three identical computer systems when one would do the job perfectly adequately, but if those three computers are on a spacecraft which will cease to function without computer control, then the extra two back-up machines may be justified in terms of effectiveness.

An interesting difference between different types of computer system is the question of the relationships in the reverse direction, i.e. 'up' the levels. For a conventional data processing system such as an accounts package, it is difficult to conceive how a system which failed at the validation level could be rated a success at the evaluation level, or how a system could be valid if it failed the verification against its specification. However, it is less clear that these restrictions apply to more advanced systems such as decision support or expert systems: if we consider a human expert, it is possible that the expert could be making a successful contribution to the organization overall (evaluation) without entirely fulfilling either their original job specification or any modified version of it (verification). This is possible for the human because specifications of human jobs tend to be imprecise by data processing standards. For example, a secretary's job description may include 'deal with personal callers', with no further indication of *how* to deal with them (offer them a cup of tea? shoot them?). However, most of this is concerned with novel aspects of the work, and at present computer systems are not capable of dealing with novel situations. We shall therefore proceed on the basis that successful verification is a necessary part of successful validation, and successful validation is in its turn a necessary part of successful evaluation.

What needs to be done?

The basic tasks involved in measuring the success of a computer system can be described very simply: establish the objectives which the organization has for the system, at all levels, and set up a programme of testing related to these objectives.

However, like our secretary's job description in the previous section, this isn't precise enough for business use. We need to look more closely at the four key elements, namely objectives, tests, metrics and judgements.

Objectives mean many different things to different people; the term is applied to statements as diverse as:

'be the U.K.'s No.1 software house'

'increase our market share'

'put a PC on the desk of every manager by the end of the year'

'calculate the payroll for up to 2000 weekly-paid employees'.

These examples vary both in the organizational task which they address, ranging from the strategic to the week-by-week operational, and in their precision. Probably only the third example would be sufficiently precise to be usable.

Our view of objectives follows that of Moravsky[3]; it is typical of the problems of terminology we have mentioned that *he* calls them goals! He identifies four characteristics which the goals/objectives must exhibit:

(i) be manifest statements (i.e. available in a written form for later reference);

(ii) be specific enough to permit objective interpretation;

(iii) focus on the receiving system (i.e. the clients/customers/users, not the providers/developers);

(iv) specify a time dimension.

These objectives need to be set at all levels, since they must cover evaluation, validation and verification.

Evaluation	Commercial issues
Validation	Computing issues (system)
Verification	Computing issues (detail)

Figure 28 Issues relevant to each level

For a computer system, we need to address both business and computing issues; there is usually a reasonably close match between the levels, what needs to be assessed, and the people responsible for the assessment, as seen in Figure 28. We have labelled the objectives at each level as performance objectives, system requirements and detailed specification respectively, to fit in with common systems development terminology (see sections 6 and 7).

Metrics and the measurement activity associated with them are probably the least contentious of our four terms; everyone will realize we mean assessing the quantifiable aspects of the system's performance. The only points to highlight are that defining what is to be measured includes choosing the metrics (i.e. the units of measurement) *and* deciding on the method to be used for measuring — including who is to do it.

Judgements are relevant in two different ways where computer systems are concerned; judgements made of the system, and judgements incorporated in the system. For an accounts package or a database system, it is feasible to assess most of its operations objectively: different, equally competent observers are unlikely to disagree about whether or not the results of a calculation are correct, or the desired record has been retrieved, or the output starts at the stated place on the VDU screen. (We are working at the verification level here.)

However, for some types of system, especially expert systems, the correctness of the system's outputs judgements may have to be related to those of the humans whose knowledge it contains. This may be the only reference available, as in credit scoring systems, for example; there is no universally applicable right decision — the only way to be certain of the right answer is to see whether the applicant does indeed make the payments on time, and if not, then it's too late! In such cases, the manager who is the 'problem owner' must set the appropriate criteria of performance at the *validation* level.

The reader may feel that there is a slight contradiction between our comments here and our earlier requirement that objectives must be specific enough to permit objective interpretation. This is not in fact a problem; the statement of objectives should only permit one interpretation, but any part of the assessment calling for a judgement is necessarily subjective. For example, one of the objectives for a system which advises customers about a company's life assurance policies may be to explain clearly and accurately the reasons for recommending a particular type of policy. 'Definitions' of clarity and accuracy could be added if necessary, so that the objective itself was unambiguous to those specifying it. However, different customers might still disagree about the clarity of the same explanation, and different experts might disagree about its accuracy.

Tests are the last of our four aspects. Hardly anyone would doubt the need for some kind of testing of a computer system before it is put into operational use, but there are problems not only with how to carry out the tests, but with what can reasonably be concluded from the test results. One school of thought — allied to the formal methods school which is mentioned in the next section — is that the only way to ensure the production of error-free software is to use languages for specification and coding which permit the correctness of the software to be proven mathematically. This is a worthy goal, and still the focus of considerable research effort, but relatively little of this work has been taken up by data processing departments so far.

Even if such a method is eventually perfected, it cannot address all the levels of performance measurement. Verification would be taken care of, as would the validation of those systems, where general agreement exists as to precisely what that system should do — for example, one which performs calculations which themselves are based on a mathematical model, such as a forecasting package. By its very nature, however, this program-proving approach cannot address either the evaluation level, or the validation of systems where some flexibility of definition exists.

In the absence of methods based on formal proof, the principal issue in testing is to balance the effort expended on testing against the resultant improvement in the quality of the system produced. Even for conventional systems, it is not unusual for testing to consume 40% of total development effort/costs, rising to as much as 80% for some safety-critical systems such as flight control and the monitoring of nuclear reactors. Despite this expenditure of effort, the combinatorial explosion which results from the loops and branches in all but the most trivial of programs means that exhaustive testing, i.e. trying all possible combinations of inputs, is impracticable given the size of business systems. The testing strategy thus needs to be developed very carefully, covering how the testing is to be carried out (almost always on more than one level), the bank of test cases to be used, and the people who are to carry out the testing. Testing is covered in much more detail in the next section.

References
1. J. W. Humble *Management by Objectives*, British Institute of Management, London, 1973.
2. R. M. O'Keefe, O. Balci and E. P. Smith 'Validating expert system performance', *IEEE Expert*, Vol. 2, No.4, pp.81-90, 1987.
3. R. L. Moravsky 'Defining goals - a systems approach', *Long Range Planning*, Vol. 10, pp.85-89, 1977.

6 | Systems development (1)

Developing new computer systems, whether they are to replace existing manual systems or existing computer systems, or even to perform entirely new tasks, is a complex management problem as well as a technical one. Essentially the difficulty lies in communication. The managers and potential users of the system understand the business reasons why the system is needed; the developers understand the technological possibilities. These understandings are, almost literally, expressed in different languages — or at least in different jargon. There's nothing inherently 'wrong' with this situation; it is the natural outcome of specialization. However, it does lead to potential misunderstandings between the developers of a computer system and their clients, and the sheer scale of computer systems development means that the effects of any mistakes which result are considerable.

So, when a computer system needs to be developed, i.e. some software needs to be written, it is not enough for the developers to do what they think is right. They need to check that the users think what they are doing is right, and this also means that they need to have ways to express what they are doing in terms which the users can understand. *N.B. Although we shall be using terms like 'developing' and even 'building' computer systems here, remember always that it is software (programs and files), not hardware, that we are talking about.*

We shall discuss systems development in two sections. The first, this one, discusses overall frameworks for the process. The following section looks in more detail at some of the tasks involved. In any system development project, whether it is your first-ever spreadsheet assignment or a multi-million pound banking system, it is always tempting to 'dive in' and start writing programs, so that there appears to be some visible sign of progress. This is nearly always a bad idea. Professor Derek Partridge coined a memorable phrase for this approach to development as RUDE, standing for Run-Understand-Debug-Edit. It should be clear to you that, even if the developers follow the advice to show the users what they are doing, there is potential for a considerable amount of wasted effort if it turns out that they have been doing the wrong thing (so they have to do it again!). Better to get it right the first time, which is entirely in tune with the philosophy of Total Quality Management that has become so popular in business recently. This means making sure that the misunderstandings are eliminated, if possible, *before* any programs are actually written.

There are three basic approaches to computer systems development:

- Structured or semi-formal methods
- Formal methods
- Evolutionary prototyping or rapid development

Structured methods are the most common in the larger system development departments, with more than 60% of systems developed using such a method. By contrast, only around 5% are developed using formal methods. Few large systems are built by evolutionary prototyping, and around 30% appear to have been built using no systematic methods at all!

When we look at smaller systems, especially the departmental PC revolution, many systems appear to be created by little more than iterative hacking, as in the classic RUDE model. There is more structure in this mess than there appears to be and, in some parts of the computing world at least, the management of evolutionary prototyping is accomplished successfully. The best example of this is the case of decision support systems (DSSs), where many of the theoreticians in the field see iterative, evolutionary development as paramount in order for the DSS to achieve its objective(s); see section 3.8.

The three approaches will now be described in turn.

Structured methods

The first successful systematic attempt to computer systems development was the life-cycle approach to systems development. There are many different versions of the Systems Development Life Cycle (SDLC), but they all share the same basic approach; the earlier a mistake or misunderstanding is noticed, the less time and effort it will take to put it right. Thus resources put into the stages before the programs are written should more than pay off when the software is actually in use, because the period for which the system is actually in use is much longer than the period it takes to develop it. As the old military saying has it: 'time spent in reconnaissance is seldom wasted'.

In the description we shall give here, the SDLC comprises 6 stages, as shown in Figure 29:

- Feasibility and requirements definition
- Analysis
- Design
- Implementation
- Testing
- Maintenance

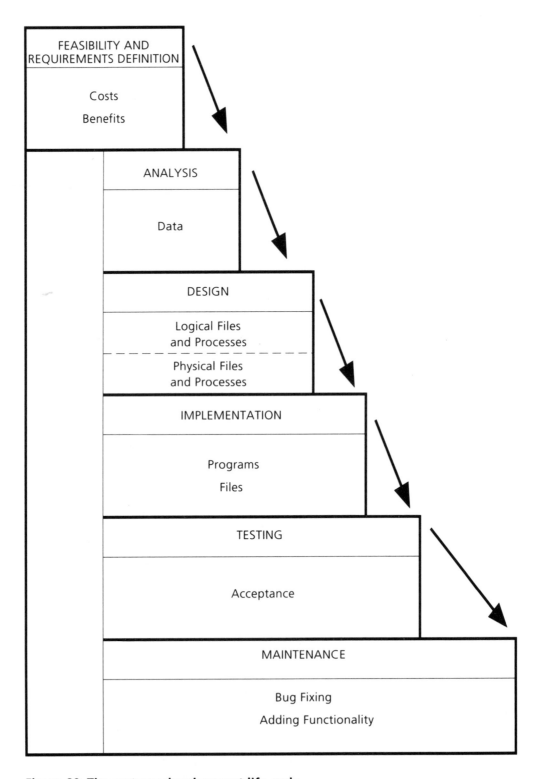

Figure 29 The systems development life cycle

Feasibility and requirements definition

The system developers, working in consultation with those commissioning the system and its intended users (who may be two different groups of people), establish the general tasks which the system is intended to perform, and the constraints (budgetary, time, etc.) on its production. This may well involve some study of existing manual or computer systems. It is important to involve those who actually use the current systems, rather than just their managers, because they are the ones who know what *really* happens, such as any informal 'short-cuts' which are more effective, or any parts of the system which are not worthwhile. This can sometimes be very different to what is supposed to happen!

The outcome of this stage should include:

- Terms of reference

- An analysis of the functional system

- A summary of the requirements for the computer system (N.B. these are 'output' requirements, in the users' terms)

- An outline description of the proposed computer system

- Estimates of costs, benefits and timescales.

Analysis

The requirements definition established in the preceding stage is used as the basis for constructing a more detailed description (usually called a specification or just 'spec') of the functionality of the system. This is achieved by modelling the relevant areas of business activity. This modelling, called Analysis, concentrates on the movement, storage and retrieval of data, and on the processes to be carried out on the data so that the required output from the activity is achieved. Tools for this include flow charts, data flow diagrams, structured English, etc. Effectively the specification describes the computer system in computing terms, whereas the requirements described it in business terms. Even so, it is important that these computing terms are still comprehensible to the clients.

Design

The specification produced in the analysis stage is used to construct a design for the complete system, including all the details of programs, files, records, etc. Design concentrates on logical and physical file structures and the processes which access them. One commonly used technique is entity-relationship analysis, or one of the many variants of it, e.g. in a book publishing example, entities might be AUTHOR, BOOK, PUBLISHER, INVOICE, WAREHOUSE, etc., with relationships such as BOOK WRITTEN-BY AUTHOR.

Implementation

The detailed design is programmed, i.e. turned into executable code, using whatever computer language or package is appropriate. Provisional versions of documentation, manuals and training material will also need to be produced at this stage, though like the code itself they may require amendment as a result of the testing process.

Testing

This process takes place at several levels. This includes testing of the individual modules or units making up the system, testing the system as a whole, testing the system under normal and unusual conditions, hands-on testing by the intended end-users, etc. The 'full system' tests will also be a test of documentation, training and operating procedures, as well as of the computerized part of the system.

Maintenance

This consists of making sure that the system runs in operational use and continues to do so for as long as is required. It includes correcting any errors which have remained undetected so far, improving the implementation of system modules where this is possible, and enhancing the functionality of the system where this is desired by the clients/users. It should be the longest of all the stages in the life-cycle as far as elapsed time is concerned.

It was because Maintenance is often, as a result, also the longest as far as person-hours of work are concerned (the Centre for Software Maintenance estimates that between 50% and 90% of the cost of a computer system over its lifetime is maintenance), that the structured approaches, also known as life-cycle or semi-formal approaches, were developed.

Whichever of the various structured design approaches is used, the purpose of structured design is to reduce the overall cost and effort involved in developing and running a computer system. This is achieved partly by introducing the structure as outlined above in order to cope with the complexity, and partly by shifting resources from maintenance and post-implementation testing to the earlier stages of the process. Standards and milestones are two crucial elements in achieving the control necessary, so that it is possible for those managing the development project to monitor and control what is happening, and for developers and clients to agree that a particular stage has been successfully completed.

The extreme version of this SDLC approach is known as the *Waterfall* model of systems development, because of the principle that once a stage has been completed, you should not need to go back to it. Looking at the way the SDLC is shown in Figure 29, it is easy to see where the name came from, with the project 'flowing down' from the top of the diagram to the bottom. However, in practice, a strict application of the Waterfall in which each stage is 'signed off' and never re-visited is likely to be too rigid. The only stage at which it can realistically be applied is the end of the feasibility and requirements definition stage, where the decision to go ahead with a computer system development (or not) is taken. In the later stages, it is simply unrealistic to expect clients to know exactly what they want before they are fully aware of what is possible. In practice, therefore, many of the Waterfall or life-cycle methods do allow for some limited form of iteration.

Structured methods, one of the rare business-driven developments in computing, have become a whole area of business in themselves, with different companies providing training courses, instruction manuals and so on. There were two reasons for this:

(i) The UK government felt that both its own systems development problems, and those of UK businesses, would be eased by having a standard approach. This would make it easier for clients to understand how computer software consultancies worked, and avoid the waste of effort involved in a systems analyst (say) learning a whole new approach every time they changed jobs. The method they commissioned was called SSADM (Structured Systems Analysis and Design Method), which is now compulsory in work for government departments.

(ii) Various computer consultancies, especially the ones who had developed SSADM for the government, saw that the sheer amount of detail involved (the documentation for SSADM version 4 runs to four volumes weighing over 9 pounds) would mean that there would be a large market for training systems developers in structured methods.

As a result, each of the structured methods (apart from SSADM) is a *proprietary* method belonging to one or two computer consultancies. Among the most common are:

- LSDM from Learmonth and Burchett
- JSD from Michael Jackson Systems (not *that* Michael Jackson!)
- Information Engineering from Arthur Young and James Martin Associates
- Method1 from Andersen Consulting
- BIS/Modus from BIS Information Systems
- Prism from Hoskyns.

Formal methods

Formal methods rely on the use of mathematical logic to accomplish the verification of the software (see section 5), i.e. to prove (in a mathematical sense) that the programs actually meet the specification produced in the analysis stage. The attractions of this are obvious. Essentially, the objective of using a formal method to specify a computer system is to improve the process of going from the agreed specification of the system to a machine-executable version of that system, by providing better means of checking for errors and by avoiding the introduction of further errors. This is (in part) achieved by producing the specification in a notation which is mathematically valid. Amongst the advantages this gives are that some of the transformations by which the code is produced from the specification may be carried out automatically, and that it may be possible to produce a rigorous proof that a program meets its specification. Unfortunately, this cannot be done with a specification written in English, or any other natural language. Instead, the specification itself has to be written in a special language; the most popular of these is called Z. As this imposes severe discipline, not to say constraint, on the systems analysis, formal methods have only found favour in applications where producing such a detailed description of the system's functionality in 'foreign' terms is organizationally and culturally feasible. The majority of these are either defence applications, safety-critical applications (nuclear power, aerospace) or both. Even in these it is not always possible to cover all aspects of the system to be specified. However, where they can be used, formal methods render iteration unnecessary once the specification has been agreed.

Evolutionary prototyping

Evolutionary prototyping, also known as iterative design, is particularly associated with the development of Decision Support Systems (see section 3.8), but has now become used for a much wider range of computer systems, where the term Rapid Application Development (or RAD) is also used. Evolutionary prototyping makes a positive virtue of iteration. It originally developed because of the difficulty of determining the requirements of a decision support system at the beginning of the project. In essence, it is a more disciplined version of RUDE. It usually proceeds along the following lines (for simplicity of description, we assume a single end-user):

1. Initial investigation by the end-user and the developer. As well as establishing a working relationship and defining the broad area in which a computer system is required, this investigation aims to identify a small sub-system as the first part to be built. It should address a part of the system which is of high interest to the end-user, and for which the nature of the computer-based support required is clear.

2. Build the system to meet the need identified in **1**, with an emphasis on simplicity and usability. For this small system, it is the equivalent of the analysis, design, implementation and testing stages of the conventional SDLC, carried out as rapidly as possible without any formal division into stages and with the involvement of the end-user throughout.

3. The end-user and the developer evaluate the system. Any changes, corrections or enhancements to be made are identified.

4. Carry out these changes/corrections/enhancements, again using the rapid analysis, design, implementation and testing approach outlined in **2**. Return to step **3**.

The iteration around stages **2**, **3**, and **4** continues until a reasonably stable system has been achieved. Note that as there is no final 'stopping criterion', the process can never be said to be finished. Some regard this as a virtue in terms of flexibility, others as a disaster in terms of use of resources! The underlying philosophy of the evolutionary prototyping approach is that of mutual learning — developers and clients working together to establish what is needed; the developers learn about the users' needs while the clients learn what is feasible for the computer system to do.

As we remarked earlier, there are now several authors who recommend the use of some kind of rapid prototyping for developing all kinds of computer system. Often this goes hand in hand with the use of 4th generation tools or languages (see section 2) to construct the system. This approach does however raise management problems which have not yet been satisfactorily answered, particularly when there are many end-users rather than one, and the manager commissioning the system is not one of the hands-on users. This raises very real issues of who takes the responsibility for what the system does.

It is important to realize, however, that rapid prototyping may have more than one meaning. The *evolutionary* prototyping which we have just described is not the only possible use of prototyping. The alternative, which in fact pre-dates the evolutionary approach, is usually called *throwaway* prototyping. Here the initial phase is very similar to evolutionary prototyping phases **1** and **2** as above, but once the prototype has been used to produce a kind of 'animated specification', it is thrown away, and the final system is designed from scratch.

Throwaway prototyping can be of considerable use within a particular stage of the conventional SDLC, especially producing the initial statement of requirements. Here the purpose of the prototype is to attempt to present the user with a realistic view of the system as it will eventually appear; users can directly experience this 'animated specification'. Communication with users, particularly the non-specialist middle management user, is considerably enhanced.

This use of prototyping is closely analogous to techniques used in civil engineering. For example, when a new building is being designed, the developers often build scale models to help finalize the design, and satisfy interested parties that the proposed structure will blend in appropriately with its surroundings.

Overall, combining the best of the structured approaches with a disciplined use of prototyping seems to offer the best way forward for business systems development at present.

7 | Systems development (2)

In this section we bring together the issues from the Organizational Aspects section 5 and the first Systems Development section 6. Bear in mind that the methods described in that section do not solve all of the problems of systems development. A particular criticism of SSADM (and indeed structured methods in general) is that:

> '...it doesn't really provide a mechanism which can aid [information systems] staff in understanding the business's broad IT requirements. There's an underlying false assumption that if you can understand enough about detailed clerical business procedures, by modelling them, using techniques such as entity life-histories, then you can use that information to build the systems needed to support business operations. But spending all your time looking at the nitty-gritty of how the business works is no way to understand the real business issues that drive computerization. SSADM assumes that by aggregating details about clerical procedures you can somehow deduce the major business issues that require the most in the way of IT support.' (Richard Heagerty, Inforem)

Clearly the only resolution of this problem is for the managers to take the responsibility for the business issues, not the system developers.

The first step is to start with the organization's business need, which must be translated into a set of performance objectives for the outcome of the project. Only then is it possible to decide whether a computer system is likely to provide an adequate 'solution'. The difficulty of this translation should not be underestimated. The decision to commission the building of a system must be taken by the problem owner(s); unless they are committed to the system, it is almost certain to fail at the evaluation level. Once the decision has been made, these objectives must be cast into a form which is appropriate for a computer system. In order to formulate the objectives for the system, we need to determine the tasks to be performed and the criteria of performance for each task.

The process must start at the evaluation level, then go down to the validation and verification levels, with the appropriate expansion of detail. It is vital to realize that this cannot all be done at the start of the project, or even at the same time. Only after some of the systems analysis has been carried out will it be possible to specify the system precisely enough to determine criteria of performance at the validation level. Equally, the metrics to be used for verification will depend to some extent on the exact hardware and software being used for the operational system; these will not be determined until the emphasis shifts from the logical design of the system to the physical design of the system.

It is inevitable that there will be some iteration between the levels, but this process needs to be controlled very carefully. In the rest of this section we will treat performance measurement and testing as if it were a simple 'once down the levels and back up again' process for clarity, as shown schematically in Figure 30, but the issue of managing iteration will be a central one which we shall comment further on in the next section.

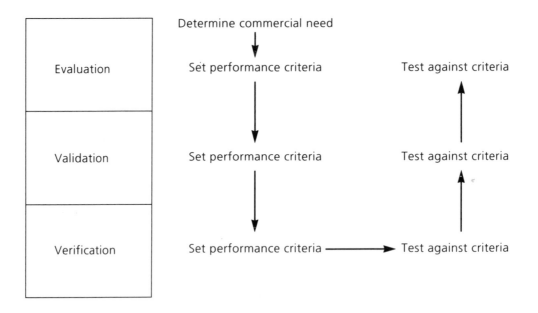

Figure 30 A 'one-shot' view of evaluation

At each of the levels, we must define the factors to be assessed in order to judge the system's performance, define who are the assessors, define metrics, timescales, measuring instruments, etc.

At the evaluation level

Begin by establishing the business need which the system must meet. This process is as much an art as a science. An appropriate analogy is perhaps that of a doctor (general practitioner) seeing a patient; the system developer is the doctor, the managers in the organization are the patients. The patient arrives with some symptoms ('*Doctor, I've got this terrible pain in my sales order processing department!*'); he may or may not understand what they are; he may or may not have his own diagnosis of the illness causing the symptoms; he may even have some idea of the treatment he wants/needs/expects! The doctor will try to establish how accurate the patient's descriptions are (does he merely feel hot, or is his temperature really higher than normal?). She will use her own observations, and if necessary and possible, carry out further tests. She may need to call for yet more tests, either by herself or by others, to be carried out at some stage in the future. Pursuing the analogy, the goal at this stage is to establish what the disease or illness is, NOT to prescribe treatment (yet). The additional difficulty faced by 'organizational doctors' is that of deciding what constitutes a 'healthy' organization as opposed to an 'ill' one.

Our suggestions here are about carrying out the process of being an 'organizational doctor', but please remember also that whilst we can present guide-lines for what needs to be done, we cannot teach you the 'bedside manner' of how to do it! It should be clear then that we see the problem of deriving criteria of performance at the evaluation level as being inextricably linked to business needs. This link is so close that the process required must aim at establishing BOTH the need and the criteria of performance. It would be a serious mistake to see this step as merely consisting of deriving appropriate criteria of performance from business needs which have already been well-established and clearly articulated. Even for 'commonplace' computer systems this is comparatively rare. For more novel or more advanced systems, three factors combine to make a joint investigation by the manager(s) who are the problem owner(s) and the potential system developer(s) imperative:

(i) the fuzziness of the issues involved;

(ii) the novelty of trying to systematize them;

(iii) the lack of familiarity of managers with the capabilities of computer systems.

Even where the basic business need is comparatively clear, for example where the organizational system concerns manufacturing process control, and the overall aim is to produce improvements in response to criticisms of operational performance, the need may have to be 'fleshed out' considerably before the project objectives can be agreed. In our example, the operational needs will have to be refined into precisely the sort of operational gains which are anticipated.

Although it would be nice to completely separate the consideration of the business need from the potential solutions, in reality this will not be the case. We have to convert the business need into a specification for the overall project task. This involves having at least a tentative idea about the sort of system to be constructed, in order to ensure that the managers are being advised by the right system development experts — there's little point in consulting a plumber when you really need an electrician! Several other aspects of this system will also need to be decided before we can accomplish this, for example:

- What is the target hardware?

- Who are the hands-on users of the computer system?

- Who are the beneficiaries of the organizational system? (May not be the same group of people as the users.)

To clarify the distinction between users and beneficiaries, suppose that we are considering a system to assist in the management of beds in a hospital ward. The hands-on users will probably be nurses, but the beneficiaries (the real customers) are neither the nurses, nor the doctors, nor the hospital administrators; they are the patients!

Specific performance objectives at this level may be divided into three categories:

Direct financial and organizational

Return on Investment. In some articles on computer systems, return on investment is the only criterion mentioned in this category. It is indeed an appropriate criterion, but only for a revenue-earning system. Most organizations will be able to decide on appropriate levels for return on investment for particular types of project, but the problem can be in determining what to include as initial investment and what to count as earnings. This applies to all projects (and is one of the reasons why organizations need accountants), but is particularly problematic when it comes to costing the time of the users involved in development.

Operational effectiveness. Improvements in the way in which operational activities are carried out may have other direct benefits than purely financial, in terms of ability to accept orders, offer shorter delivery times, introduce new products, etc. It is under this heading that the major part of the considerable benefits attributed by DEC to the use of the R1/XCON expert system come (see section 3.11). The current buzz-phrase for this is 'gaining competitive advantage', but that does not necessarily make it any easier to measure.

Cost-saving. Many organizational activities are administrative, rather than directly earning revenue. Such systems support the primary activities of the organization rather than carrying them out. Financial improvements may result from improved efficiency or by changing the cost structure.

Cost-minimizing. Some organizational activities cannot be directly related to the organization's outputs at all, such as various statutory duties, social facilities for employees, etc. In this case the likely choice would be the cheapest adequate system, either in terms of the initial investment or in net present value terms.

Assessment against these financial and operational criteria should be carried out by the managers responsible for the system and their financial advisors.

Quality of decision-making

Does the computer system function well enough for the organization's business need? In other words, is it working in the real environment, as opposed to any tests which might have been carried out at the validation level? This will include both the question of whether it is adequately knowledgeable, and whether it is usable by the people for whom it was intended. It does not matter how well a computer system performs in tests, if the organization lacks the confidence to trust its operation and recommendations in real-life. (This has been a particular problem with some types of medical decision support systems.) Thus some of the measures under this heading will be quantitative metrics, and others qualitative judgements. *As with a human, we are asking not just 'do they know enough to do the job?', but 'do they fit in?' The difference between this and the similar aspect at the validation level corresponds to the difference between judging a human's job performance and assessing their qualifications.*

Quantitative assessment against this type of criterion should be by the managers responsible for the organizational system, advised by the computer system builder where necessary. Qualitative assessments should be by the managers, the domain experts, and the hands-on users, and perhaps by other staff who interact with the computer system indirectly. The assessment should, when appropriate, include confirmation from the intended beneficiaries of the system.

Indirect (opportunity) benefits

Current computer systems do not know very much about the world as a whole, and in that sense are considerably inferior to humans. Thus many computer systems are not intended to replace humans, but rather to support them by freeing their time or improving the quality of their performance. Evaluation of the computer system must therefore include an attempt to assess these opportunity benefits. This is NOT in terms of time freed — that is a validation issue; the system may give a manager or a clerk more time, but cannot guarantee that anything useful is done in that time. At this level, we must look for actual 'useful' activities which the people are carrying out which they did not do before, or new skills which have been acquired as a result of the computer system. We would recommend that the approach to this aspect is qualitative/subjective, rather than quantitative. Anything with even a hint of work study or job evaluation is likely to sour the climate for the implementation of the computer system, which involves quite enough problems as it is!

Assessment against this criterion should be by the managers responsible, with the assistance of the hands-on users.

The three categories are summarized in Figure 31. All units of measurement and measuring instruments should be those which are determined by the organization's business needs, such as standard financial indicators, market research methods and human performance appraisal techniques. At this level, the fact that we are using a computer system does not affect the nature of the measurements. Specific details of such techniques are beyond the scope of this book, but may be found in any good management text.

Financial	Quantitative, but with some subjectivity over what to include
Quality of Decision-making	Both quantitative and qualitative
Opportunity Benefits	Qualitative

Figure 31 Measurement factors at the evaluation level

At the validation level

As with the evaluation level, we must define the factors to be assessed in order to judge the system's performance. The difference at this level is that the system requirements must be much more detailed than the performance objectives, and that computing and domain issues play a much larger part.

What to validate?
Is the concentration to be on the process or on the end-result? For some types of computer system, for example a computer-based learning system, there is only a process to assess, since no definite outputs such as decisions are reached. It might be thought, at the other extreme, that if a system does produce a definite decision or recommendation, then that alone should suffice for validation, but this is not always the case. Especially in the case of decision support or expert systems, intermediate advice and justification are often given,

as well as the 'final answer', and it makes sense to assess all of these if possible. After all, a system which produces a result like the proverbial 'rabbit out of a hat' is unlikely to be acceptable unless it is for a very well-structured task.

Who are to be the validators?

Any trials of the whole system for the purposes of validation are meaningless unless carried out by the people who are to be the end-users of the system. The system developers will of course need to be closely monitoring the trials, but the element of judgement involved where computer systems are concerned renders it vital that we use the 'right' people for the tests. In addition, it is important that where there are many potential users, as wide a range as possible are incorporated in the trials.

Where the computer system can be separated into parts for the purposes of validation, some of which do not involve the end-users, then it may be possible for the system developers alone to validate such parts. For example, this may include checking that the system correctly uses graphics when required. We would expect that parts which can be validated in this manner would be those which are the most 'standard'. The nearer we come to the judgement of humans, the more careful we must be to involve the end-users.

Example (due to Hugh Dorans): an expert system for classifying rock samples was being developed, with the intention of aiding geology students. Geologists have developed many terms to describe the appearance of different rock samples under the microscope. However, new geology students cannot relate these terms to what they see. Thus the standard classifications could not be used as the basis of the system's knowledge unless they were first taught to the students.

Where judgements have to be made about the system, then obviously humans who are knowledgeable about the domain in which it operates must be involved. No-one else, even the manager who commissioned the system, is qualified to do the job (and remember, many people do have to manage business systems which they themselves do not fully understand).

Because of the judgements involved, the manager must also be involved at the validation level as the final arbiter who resolves disagreements.

Timescales

The computer system literature leaves us with a contradiction of views between those who feel that a computer system should immediately perform at the levels expected, and those who feel that it takes time to achieve such levels of performance; the latter usually goes hand-in-hand with a recommendation for parallel running of the new system alongside the old. This issue overlaps evaluation (which can only be done once the system has been delivered) and validation. Our view is that validation tests should begin as any working version of the computer system exists. This is one of the aspects where properly-managed iteration is essential. It is much easier for the developers to refine a computer system than to work entirely in the abstract.

Measuring instruments

At this level, the units of measurement are determined principally by general issues about expertise and system performance. Unfortunately, this is not without problems: a brief discussion of the problems of validating the knowledge of humans will help to clarify this.

Many professions require the passing of certain examinations before membership is granted. Yet the pass-mark is nowhere near 100% (at least in those cases with which we are familiar). Similarly, few organizations would fire a human manager for the occasional mistake. As an aside, our earlier point about assessing the process is backed up by the way in which most examination papers are marked for the quality of the argument or method and not just the 'right' answer or conclusions. So, beyond the purely mechanical aspects of system performance, how good does a computer system for (say) assessing loan applications have to be?

Our advice here is to concentrate on the beneficiary's view of the computer system, and of other ways of carrying out the same task (e.g. unaided human, paper-based system, other computer system if available). Metrics and judgements should be related primarily to the outputs provided for the beneficiary. Note that where the requirements of the system relate to ease of maintenance or amendment, the effective beneficiary will be the maintenance programmer, the system developer and perhaps the end-user.

Metrics (quantitative validation)

Here we are comparing the performance of the computer system (usually in terms of calculation, items retrieved, final decision or recommendations) with known performance. We have already discussed how the 'correct' answers may themselves rely on judgement; alternatively we may be able to assess the right decision independently, say in the case of a calculation, prediction or forecast. It is up to the manager to decide on the 'pass-mark' for these tests, which will normally be less than 100%, as we argued earlier. As with any performance comparison, the sampling implicit in the deliberate or chance selection of test cases makes it essential to use statistical methods to compare actual and desired performance. Any good statistical textbook will give an introduction to such methods.

Judgements (qualitative validation)

Again it is necessary for the manager and the system developer to agree on the appropriate standards which the computer system is expected to reach. The subjective nature of this task may make it necessary for these standards to be determined early enough to be written into any contract between the two parties.

At the verification level

In principle, this is almost a mechanistic task. We are dealing with functionality against specification, looked at in information technology terms. It is easy to state what needs to be done, but there can be problems in actually *doing* it because of the sheer scale of the task involved. Over the years, considerable effort has been expended on developing *test harnesses* and test data banks for common computer languages and applications. As you would expect, this 'testing equipment' is better developed for languages which are more widely used, used in larger systems and used in safety-critical applications. This may affect decisions taken about which software is to be used for the system, back at the validation level. Detailed testing at this level is a mater for the developers rather than the managers, although there is a great deal to be said for having hands-on users involved in the testing as soon as possible. The testing must also take account of both normal and abnormal operating conditions, although it is difficult to cope with *all* eventualities (see section 9).

Summary

Unless your concern is solely with research and development computer systems, then your computer system must be built in response to a business need in the organization. Its success (or otherwise) should therefore be measured on that basis.

This involves comparing the system's performance with its objectives at each of three levels: evaluation, validation and verification.

We have set out our recommendations as to how to do this, drawing on our experience and on lessons from related fields. On the whole, there is still surprisingly little effort put into formally measuring the success of business computer systems, and so these ideas may yet need modification in the future, particularly when it comes to methods for validation.

8 | People

Way back in the Business Computing Essentials section, we identified various roles relevant to the use of computer systems. In this section we look more closely at the different responsibilities and job titles which you will find in a computing department or company. Our reason for saying 'department or company' is that the most basic choice facing any user organization is whether to acquire its computer software in-house, in a department that may be called Information Systems or one of a dozen other titles, or to go outside to a computer consultancy or software house.

Very briefly, the arguments in favour of these two options run as follows. In-house staff are loyal to the company, understand the way that it works, are familiar with the existing computer systems, and are likely to be on hand in the future if something goes wrong. External staff bring a fresh view, can be selected to have more experience with the specific technology needed for a new system, and are more directly paid for what they deliver. External staff tend to be more expensive than in-house staff for any given task, but on the other hand in-house staff (and their offices etc.) represent a continuing overhead to the organization. The figures in the Money section (4) show that the balance at present is still very much in favour of in-house staff; expenditure on in-house staff salaries is more than double that on bought-in software, programming and consultancy.

Whether working for users or for a software consultancy, computing staff have their own hierarchy, just like any other profession. Computing is not quite like other professions, though. To begin with, unlike say accountancy or the law in the UK, there are no restrictions on entry; anyone is legally permitted to set themselves up as a one-person computing consultancy. There is however a widely-recognized system of professional qualifications, especially those offered by the British Computer Society, which is the largest professional body and now has a Royal Charter. Other professional organizations include the Institute of Data Processing Managers, while computing professionals have now even achieved recognition alongside much older professions as one of the guilds of the City of London, the Worshipful Company of Information Technologists. Perhaps a more significant point however concerns the absence of a universally agreed name for the profession! The term 'software engineering' was deliberately coined in order to give an impression of reliability similar to that evoked — at least for some people — by other engineering disciplines. The credit is usually given to Professor Tony Hoare, who suggested the term at a 1968 conference under the auspices of NATO. This was in response to a profession (perhaps a craft would have been a more accurate term at the time) which had earned a reputation for delivering systems incomplete, after time and over budget. Twenty-five years on, engineering has definitely fallen in social status, at least in the UK, and while the term software engineering is in use, it has not gained universal acceptance. The labels 'computing professional' and 'data processing professional' are just as common as 'software engineer', and many people who work in computing would go down one level to their job title and say 'I am a systems analyst' or 'I am a computer programmer' rather than attempting to refer to the profession at all. Note however that suitably qualified and experienced members of the British Computer Society can now achieve the status of Chartered Engineer, so the engineering link is still strong.

If we do look at the job titles amongst operators, developers and suppliers in computing, the first point is that there is no entirely standard terminology. One reason for this is that many computing departments are actually quite small. Around 75% of computing departments have fewer than 10 staff, and the average number of staff in a department is also slightly less than 10. Not surprisingly, there is rather a difference between the structure of a department in one of the major banks, with perhaps several hundred staff, and a two-person department in a small manufacturing company. This makes it harder to characterize what a 'typical' computing department is.

Figure 32 shows the breakdown of computing/data processing staff according to their function. Although systems development staff form the largest single group at 32%, it may be seen that those responsible for developing new systems are actually outnumbered by those whose principal concern is with supporting the current systems (operations, data preparation and technical support, a total of 40.1%). Operations and data preparation are usually regarded as being clerical-level tasks, and those who carry them out are paid accordingly.

The operators are the people who actually run the system. Their responsibilities range from starting up the machine in the morning (if it does not run 24 hours a day), through loading magnetic tapes and disks when needed, keeping the printers supplied with the right sort of paper, to monitoring the jobs which the system is running at any time and taking back-ups of the data and software (see section 9). Many large systems do actually run 24 hours a day (see section 3.9); night-shift computer operations can be a very lonely job indeed!

Data preparation is still a major activity, and basically involves entering data from the keyboard. Although there have been great advances in electronic communications, most interactions between organizations and their individual customers still take place on paper or over the telephone. For example, if you order an item from a mail-order catalogue, whether in writing or over the telephone, someone has to type the relevant data into the computer (over the telephone you can often hear the rattle of the keys at the other end as you place your order!). Efforts are being made to automate some of these processes, but human data preparation will be around for a fair while yet.

The average manager in a user department or organization should not need to interact very much with operations or data preparation staff directly, but rather with their 'bosses' in the management of the data processing department. The brief descriptions given above will therefore suffice for the purposes of this book.

The 'professionals' in computing are those in development (which also includes maintenance, as set out in sections 6 and 7), technical support and some (but not all) of the management positions. Explaining the differences in the names of the posts they hold is a near-impossible task; the Computer Users Year Book annual salary survey identifies 9 different management job titles in computing, each of which applies to at least 2000 people in the UK, and a further 9 development job titles, each applying to at least 3000! These are listed in Table 11. In practice, many of the differences in job title are for internal political reasons within the organization concerned, rather than anything to do with their function. We will, however, attempt to give an outline of the different jobs here.

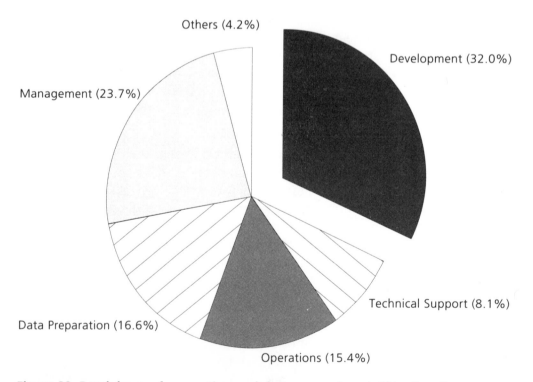

Figure 32 Breakdown of computing and data processing staff by function

Table 11 Job titles in computing

Management staff

Head of Management Services

DP Manager

Chief Systems Analyst

Chief Programmer

Chief Analyst/Programmer

Operations Manager

Technical Support Manager

Communications Manager

User Support Manager

Development staff

Business Analyst

Senior Systems Analyst

Systems Analyst

Senior Programmer

Programmer

Junior Programmer

Senior Analyst/Programmer

Analyst/Programmer

Hardware/Technical Planning Analyst

Source: *Computer Users Year Book*

The most basic, or easily identified, types of post are three in number: data processing manager, systems analyst and programmer, in order of seniority. Describing in detail what a manager has to manage is beyond the scope of this book, but a DP manager's work is likely to include responsibility for the internal running of the department, the performance of current systems and negotiations with user managers about new systems or enhancements to existing ones. The systems analyst's main responsibilities are for the analysis of existing systems, and the analysis and design of new ones (see sections 6 and 7 for much more detail). The programmer, as you would expect, writes the programs. Both programmer and systems analyst are involved in testing, the responsibility shifting from the former to the latter as the testing moves from the lowest level of modules to that of the system as a whole.

Most of the senior, chief and junior posts do not need further explanation, being ways of sub-dividing groups of otherwise similar staff in larger departments. Note that the relevance of these is almost entirely for the computing department's internal purposes such as the way it organizes itself and the career development of the people within it. The actual status of the programmers or analysts assigned to a project for you, as a business user or manager, should not need to concern you. Similarly, posts like Operations Manager, in a department with many operations staff (and probably several machines), are more or less self-explanatory.

Two types of job title do need a bit more explanation, however: the analyst/programmer and the business analyst.

The analyst/programmer carries out almost all of the activities in the systems development life-cycle, and is more likely to be found in any of the following circumstances:

● In projects involving maintenance or small enhancements to existing systems.

● In the development of personal computer-based systems for standalone use, rather than networked PCs or mainframes.

● In small departments.

● In small systems development, especially of systems such as decision support systems.

The proportion of analyst/programmers has increased with the proliferation of PC-based systems, and with the rise in software tools to help the software engineer, so that some of the effort involved shifts from programming to analysis and design.

The business analyst's major responsibility is in the earliest stages of system development, the feasibility study and identification of the business requirements. As the name implies, an analyst concentrates on the business aspects instead of the computing ones, and thus plays a key role in any business process re-engineering (that buzz-word again!) which may be required.

9 | Security

There are three aspects of security which should concern those responsible for managing business computing: security of equipment, security of access to the computer system, and security of data. In each case, steps need to be taken to deal with both accidental and deliberate threats to the security of the computer systems. We shall deal with each in turn, although naturally the three are closely interlinked.

a) Security of equipment

The most visible security issues concern the equipment itself; chiefly the hardware, but also to some extent the software. The principal deliberate threat here is theft, whilst the main accidental ones are damage and loss of power.

Taking the accidental threats first, large computers are extremely complex in both electronic and mechanical terms. They function best at a constant temperature and in a room where there is as little dirt around as possible. For large mainframes, it makes economic sense to put them in a special room with a controlled environment featuring air conditioning and the filtering-out of dust particles. Many older mainframes actually produced a lot of heat themselves, and some had to be water-cooled, rather like cars have to have radiators. Modern personal computers will function quite happily in a normal office environment, but even so care needs to be taken. It's a good idea not to subject them to extreme heat or cold; one of the authors had a PC 'clone' in his office which would not work properly on winter mornings until it had had time to warm up a bit!

Disk technology, with the read/write heads skimming just above the surface of the disk, is rather like flying a jet fighter at twice the speed of sound 20 feet (6 metres) off the ground. That's the easy bit. It's counting the blades of grass passing underneath which is difficult! Smoking near a PC has the potential to ruin the disk drives, and most organizations do not allow it. Eating and drinking are not advisable either, and most university computing workshops ban those as well. There are no firm figures, but anecdotal evidence would suggest that more damage is caused to office computers by spilt coffee than anything else! Incidentally, although the power consumption of a modern PC is many orders of magnitude less than that of a 1960s mainframe, problems of overheating still surface from time to time, most recently with some of the first computers based on the new Pentium chip from Intel.

Having persuaded your staff not to mistreat the computer, it is also worth looking at the question of the power supply. No power equals no computing. There are portable computers which will run for a few hours on batteries, but as no-one knows when the power is going off, these are only really useful for the applications on them already. Where the functioning of the computer system is crucial to the business, it is likely to be worth investing in some form of back-up power supply. For any period longer than an hour or so, this will mean having your own stand-by generators available; some organizations, such as hospitals, will already have them anyway. Generators come expensive, and can only be justified for systems which *must* keep running. More commonly, the need is to maintain power for long enough to turn the system off gracefully, so that there is no loss of data. This is the territory of the so-called uninterruptible power supply (UPS). UPSs are battery-based systems which are connected between the power supply and the computer. In normal operation, the computer actually runs from the battery of the UPS, which is constantly being charged up by the mains supply. Thus there is no interruption in the power supply to the computer if the mains supply fails; it just means the battery is no longer being charged up. The cost of such systems ranges from just under £1000 up to several thousand pounds, depending on how much power is needed and whether it is for a few minutes or a few hours. Even if a business has stand-by generators, it will also need a UPS to cover the period while the generators are starting up. There are also cheaper 'UPSs' which strictly are not uninterruptible at all. In these, the mains power runs the computer through the UPS and, separately, charges the battery; the UPS detects when there is a problem with the mains power supply, and cuts in the battery after 3 or 4 milliseconds. This is a fairly long time in computing terms, so whatever is being done at the precise moment the power goes off may go wrong, but it is short enough not to have the effect of switching the machine off.

UPSs also have another useful function: protecting the equipment from fluctuations in the mains supply. The UK has a very reliable mains supply, even by European standards, but there are variations, especially in bad weather. For example, a drop in voltage which makes the lights flicker may be enough to affect the operation of a computer. Running the supply through a UPS will remove these fluctuations. These problems are more acute than many computer users realize, because they tend to occur most in the evenings, when demand for electricity is at its highest and has its most sudden variations (linked to popular TV shows). Fewer computers are in use during the evenings than during the day, but those which are, are usually for the applications which are most critical to the business.

Turning to deliberate threats, the main problem is theft. Theft of hardware was actually not a major problem before the arrival of the personal computer, because until then most computers were in a special room, often with an operator present 24 hours a day, and the average piece of equipment required at least two people to move it. (*Although there was one notable case where thieves found out that a mainframe computer was due to be returned to the manufacturer and succeeded in stealing it by impersonating the transport firm, complete with a truck fitted with a mobile hoist!*) However, the personal computer is (relatively) easy to move, and is far and away the most valuable item in the average office. There have even been claims that gangs of thieves were stealing computers to order, based on reported thefts where only the newest-model personal computers were taken. There are no specific answers to computer theft, except to ensure that the business's insurance and building security are adequate. It is not unusual to find the machines in personal computer workshops in universities, schools and colleges physically chained to the wall or tables, though!

Most of what we have said in this section has been about hardware, because the threats to the software once it is installed on the hardware are exactly the same as those we shall cover under Security of Data. However, there is one threat to businesses which is worth mentioning, namely the illegal use of software, or *software piracy*, as it is known.

As with hardware theft, illegal copying of software used to be extremely rare in the days when an organization might have at most a handful of machines and there was no mass market for packaged software. However, software piracy is now a major problem in the personal computer market. It has two sources: one is the 'organized law-breaking' operation, as with fake Rolex watches; the other is made up of individuals (and even some companies) who feel 'if it is *possible* to make my own copy, then why shouldn't I?', as with illegal copies of video-tapes, or indeed the controversy over home taping of records and CDs.

Somewhat surprisingly, it is the latter source — making multiple copies of a legally-purchased original — which constitutes the larger threat. A UK initiative against this is the Federation Against Software Theft (FAST), which was set up in 1984. It works in close collaboration with its international equivalent, the Business Software Alliance. Both groups were originally formed by software suppliers to protect their own legitimate interests, and their membership now also includes large users such as Marks and Spencer, and Boots. One of FAST's first achievements was in helping to secure the passing of the Copyright (Computer Software) Amendment Law by Parliament in 1985. FAST has successfully instituted various 'raids' on user organizations believed to be using illegally copied software, including (in 1991) Mirror Group Newspapers and the London Borough of Greenwich (*Computing*, 21 January 1993). Both of these cases were eventually settled out of court. To give some idea of the magnitude of the problem, the Business Software Alliance looks at figures for hardware and software sales, and then performs the following 'calculation': most PC software is packaged, or written using a package, so it would be reasonable to expect around three applications per PC to be sold on average. On this basis, the UK's figure of 1.39 packages sold per PC in 1992, which translates to an estimated 46% legal software, is the best in Europe, although the USA does rather better! Figure 33 shows the figures for various European countries and for the USA; no 1992 figures for Eastern Europe were available, but those from earlier years were considerably worse than even Italy or Spain. A survey specifically of Macintoshes in the UK showed 1.39 illegal packages for every legal one, which is consistent with the above figures.

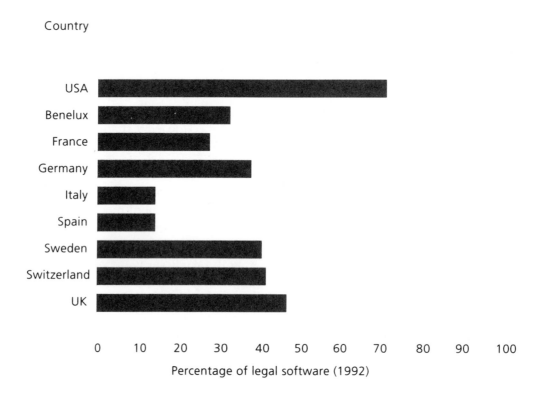

Figure 33 Legal and illegal software in use by country

The Business Software Alliance estimates that these statistics translate into an annual loss of around US$5 billion in Europe for software vendors, but the 1992 picture did show an improvement on that of previous years — due in part, no doubt, to the influence of some 100 legal actions instituted by the Business Software Alliance in 10 different European countries during the year!

The only way managers can prevent software piracy in their own organization is by making sure that they know what software is loaded on each machine. This is no easy task when these machines are physically distributed across the organization, and may even involve spot checks on what software is in use. There are even specific software packages available to help record the necessary information. Probably the best answer is to educate all users to have more respect for the time and money invested in development which is represented by the copyright in computer software.

b) Security of access

Given that the system is there and functioning, the next question is: who is permitted to use it? When interactive computing arrived, the operators lost the effective sole control of the computer which they had previously had. The system now had to cope with multiple users as well. The problem thus arose of making sure that each user only accessed the parts of the system which they were permitted to, irrespective of the other tasks which the computer was doing at the time. This was (and is) usually done by a system of user identifiers and passwords, which constitutes part of the operating system of the computer. The user identifiers, also known as usernames, log-ins, sign-ons or userIDs, are publicly known, so as to allow communication between users, identification of file ownership and so on. A user identifier might look like JSE1 or LEWISCD or, more cryptically, ABS9117. The second element, the password, is the one which really provides the security. It is known only to the user, not even to the operators of the system. The Personal Identification Number or PIN system used with credit cards is derived from computer password systems. For obvious reasons, we will not give you examples of what our passwords might be, but the general issue of password choice is worthy of some discussion. A password should really not be a word which is in the dictionary, because spelling checkers mean that computerized dictionaries are widely available, and industrial espionage might well make it worth the time and trouble of writing a program to try all the words in the dictionary. A password should not be too short, for the same reason of trial-and-error access as above, but also should not be too long (say about 10 characters), because for security reasons it does not appear on the screen as you type it, and so the longer the password, the more likely you are to make a mistake in typing it in. Commonly-used passwords in English-speaking countries which fail to meet these requirements include PASSWORD, SEX and FRED (look at the keyboard carefully to see the reason for the latter). Proper names of close friends, relations or pets are reasonable choices as a start, but not for highly secure operations, as they can be guessed by people who know you well enough; this was a key element in the plot of the mid-1980s movie 'War Games'. Some systems now will not allow you to choose a password which is in the dictionary.

Password-controlled security was not a major concern in the early days of microcomputers. The facilities were available, but physical security of the hardware in the form of a lock which required a key to switch the computer on was probably more effective in the rare cases where it was needed. However, as networks of PCs become ever more common, the username and password issue has become familiar to PC users as well. Indeed, a modern mainframe or PC network system may well have several levels of security passwords. This brings its own problems, since the more passwords a person must remember, the harder it becomes to remember them all. The computing specialists in a large organization might easily have to deal with 20 or more forgotten passwords each week. Since the user-selected passwords are even secure from the operators, no-one can actually find out what a forgotten password is. Solving this problem usually involves those responsible for managing access using their higher 'security clearance' to set a temporary password to allow the (otherwise helpless) user back into the system.

An interesting alternative to a key-operated lock is that of an electronic device which plugs into one of the sockets at the back of the PC. This device, called a *dongle,* has been adopted more widely for a different type of security — preventing software piracy, especially the unauthorized use of software packages by making several illegal copies of a legally-purchased original. The package will not function unless the dongle is in place. This allows the taking of back-up copies to protect your data and programs, but prevents you from using more than one copy at a time — an arrangement generally seen as equitable.

Despite all these precautions, or more accurately, because they are not used properly, unauthorized access, commonly known as *hacking,* does take place. Unauthorized access by itself is a relatively minor problem except in the rare cases when it prevents an authorized user from accessing the system, but it usually goes hand-in-hand with a breach of data security as well, which can be a major problem indeed. Contrary to popular belief, most hackers are company employees, working during office hours!

The full extent of hacking is usually not reported, especially by companies in the finance sector, to save the embarrassment and loss of confidence which might result. Thus almost all of the cases which are made public come from the public sector or from education. To give a small example, an employee in the housing department of the borough of Hammersmith and Fulham in London transferred £67,000 to a bogus building society account, having broken into the payments system using the password of another manager. He made payments which appeared to be to a genuine building firm, disguising the source of the instructions. He was caught when building society staff became suspicious about the amounts of cash he was withdrawing. Note that it was not a system failure here, but a human failure: the other manager's password should have been kept secret.

Hacking can sometimes even be done with the blessing of an employer, for reasons of industrial espionage, as in the recent allegations that British Airways' staff hacked into the Virgin Atlantic passenger reservation system, which was actually held on BA's own hardware.

Most of these cases are dealt with internally, and so receive little or no publicity; by contrast, the few cases of unauthorized access by the archetypal 'mad computer hacker' over public networks have to be dealt with in court, and are publicized accordingly. We shall discuss this further in the next sub-section.

c) Security of data

Much of the data and programs held on computer systems are crucial to the functioning of the business concerned. It has been estimated in the USA that of all firms which suffer a major computer catastrophe, 85% go out of business within 18 months. There are essentially two aspects to maintaining the security of your data: one is making sure that it may be accessed when it is needed; the other is making sure that it is correct, i.e. it has not been corrupted, or altered improperly. Most of the threat of improper alteration can be removed by controlling access adequately as in the previous sub-section. Making sure that the data is available and uncorrupted needs to be tackled at two levels: one is a whole system level, often termed *disaster recovery*; the other is the local, day-to-day operational level. These levels are, however, linked, as will become clear.

Taking the second one first, the key to security of data at the day-to-day level is the frequent taking of back-up copies. Indeed, one of the characteristics of an operating system which concerns the technical specialists is how easy it is to back-up the data and restore from the back-up copies when necessary. In a mainframe environment, taking and storing back-up copies of the data is the responsibility of the computer operators. In most commercial organizations this will be done on at least a daily basis. The same principles should apply to personal computer systems, but it is well-known that users often pay little heed to them (another potential hidden cost of PC use). One problem is that mainframe back-ups are typically made outside normal working hours, which is not possible for the average PC.

PC networks offer the chance for centralized backing-up of data to take place, but this raises an interesting problem. The 'obvious' way to store data on a PC network is for the programs used by everyone to be stored on the central file server, but for an individual's own files to be on his or her own machine. However, the central file server's files are the only ones which the network administrator can back up, so there is a lot to be said for having a user's files also on the file server, rather than on the hard disk of the desktop PC. This is such a drastic change in working practices for some people that it is not yet widely accepted.

At the very least, any individual working on a personal computer should ensure that they have at least two copies of every important file, on separate disks (preferably kept in separate rooms as a precaution against fire or theft, but few people do this). Whether you are word-processing, using a spreadsheet, or whatever, it is also advisable to save your work every ten minutes or so, to avoid short-term loss of data by simply making a mistake.

If you do manage to back up your personal computer's data every day, and either take one copy home with you, or leave it in a fire-proof safe, you are on your way towards having a disaster recovery program. Disaster recovery is actually concerned with all three aspects of security as discussed in this section. It does not really matter whether your inability to access the data on your usual system is caused by a processor failure on your machine or an earthquake wrecking the building which used to house it. In either case, you need an alternative system (and a copy of the data which was on the old one) in order for the business to continue functioning. Thus, the back-up copies of data in a large organization may well include a second copy which is stored on a different site altogether in case of major fire, earthquake or similar disaster. The organization will also need a machine to use in the short term. Some companies, including some hardware vendors, offer such services for a fee which is effectively an insurance premium. Other organizations, especially in the public sector, have reciprocal arrangements. Many financial organizations actually run two similar systems in different places. For example, one major bank's customer accounts are supported by two systems which in normal circumstances cover the southern and northern halves of the country respectively. If necessary, either system could take on the whole task (obviously with a slight drop in the level of service).

Many organizations in the City of London have had their disaster recovery procedures tested only too well by recent terrorist bombings. To give an example of successful disaster recovery from a different cause, Lancaster City Council lost its mainframe to a weekend power failure in October 1992. Running the monthly payroll was deemed to be top priority, as it was due to be finished on Monday. They brought in their plan arranged with an external bureau to use a machine in Leeds, so that by 10 am on Monday they were re-building the system from Friday's back-up tapes. By lunchtime the staff in Lancaster's offices were in contact with, and able to use, the system in Leeds, and the payroll information reached BACS (the banks' automated payments system) just before the 8 pm deadline. Meanwhile, back at the office, North-Western Electricity had installed a portable generator to keep them going until Tuesday lunchtime when power was restored.

The last point worth mentioning under the security of data concerns *computer viruses* and the like; programs deliberately written in an attempt to damage or destroy the data on other people's computer systems. We do not need to go into the details here of the different ways in which different types of program cause problems; the computer virus will be enough for our purpose. A computer virus is a program which does one or both of the following:

- It copies itself onto any disk used in a machine which it has 'infected'

- It corrupts all files of a certain type, often in a supposedly humorous way, such as having all the letters on the screen suddenly fall to the bottom in a heap.

Computer viruses got their name from the first of these, which means they are 'catching'; if a floppy disk with a virus on it is put into a personal computer, the virus will affect the hard disk of that machine, and then any other floppy disk put into the same machine. Free computer games are a common way of distributing viruses to the unsuspecting public! Viruses were unknown in pre-personal computer days, simply because the actual magnetic disks and tapes were under the control of the operators. They are not as serious a problem as the national press has tried to make out, but most organizations now take the precaution of investing in one of the anti-virus software packages (or even hardware) now available, which can detect viruses and 'cure' infected files and disks. The best way to avoid virus problems is not to use any 'dubious' disks, or any machines which might have used dubious disks, but in some environments (e.g. a student one), this is easier said than done. Bear in mind that if you back-up an infected disk by simply copying the files, the virus will also be on the back-up!

Part E
HARDWARE (2)

For most people interested in business computing, we believe that the detailed hardware sections which follow will prove to be less necessary than the others in the book. Nevertheless, we have included them for completeness, as a source of reference material for some of the sections, and also for those amongst our readers who are more interested in the technology itself. We would, however, not advise you to read through these sections in detail until the need arises!

10 | Input devices

There has to be a way of telling a computer what to do, and giving it the data required to do it. Effectively there are only two sources of input: human beings, and other computers or electronic systems. We concentrate for the most part in this section on devices for human input.

10.1 Keyboard

The standard input device to a computer is the keyboard. Figure 34 shows a typical personal computer keyboard layout. All keyboards in the English-speaking world use the traditional QWERTY layout for character keys (as with the traditional typewriter) but in addition also have:

- 10 or 12 function keys labelled F1, F2, etc. These are special keys with specific functions usually controlled by the applications software. Thus, for instance, convention makes the function key F1 the HELP key for virtually all application packages.

- A numeric keypad similar to that on a calculator, with just the numeric characters 0 to 9 with the (.), full stop or period, for professional typists' input of numerical data.

- Special keys such as Esc (Escape), Ctrl (Control), Alt (Alternative) which are usually used in conjunction with standard character keys — these effectively mean each key can carry out more functions, like the way the shift key on an ordinary typewriter gives capital letters.

- Cursor (or arrow) keys for positioning the screen cursor.

Unfortunately the layout of the additional keys is not yet standard, which doesn't help either users who are struggling to find where (say) the PageUp key is, or those writing software packages (there is no point in making the F12 key mean Print in a program intended for a computer which does not have an F12 key on its keyboard).

A microcomputer keyboard is always connected to a microcomputer through a special *port* (socket) with a special plug so that there is no chance of using the wrong one.

The QWERTY typewriter keyboard is named after the first few keys on the top row of letters. This keyboard layout was devised in the 1870s, specifically to slow the typist (in those days also known as a 'typewriter'!) down, because if

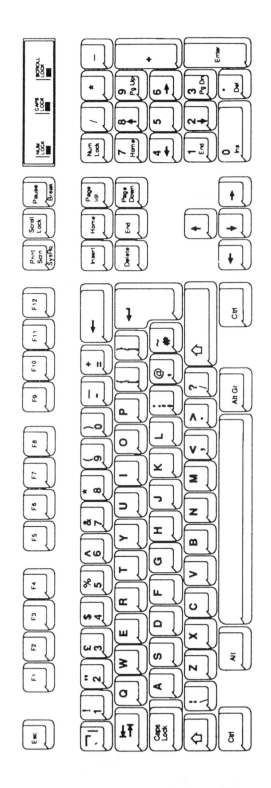

Figure 34 A typical personal computer keyboard layout

one types too fast on a mechanical typewriter, the keys will jam. So, for example, the most common letters such as e and t are on the top line and the left-hand side. Alternative keyboard layouts, usually claiming improvements of around 30% in efficiency, have been suggested over the years, but the sheer scale of the investment in this de facto standard has prevented any change, despite attempts to break the mould with different layouts and even entirely different shapes of keyboard. We appear to be stuck with QWERTY unless and until a completely different method such as speech or pen input takes over!

Note also that in non-English-speaking countries the order of the letters on the keyboard is different; the French keyboard, for example, starts AZERTY rather than QWERTY.

10.2 Mouse

A mouse is a specialized input device used especially with graphics packages and increasingly also with spreadsheets and other applications, particularly with a graphical user interface (see section 1.2) such as Windows. It was given its name because the lead connecting to the computer looks like the long thin tail of a mouse. By physically moving the mouse on a flat surface, the user can achieve more speed and flexibility in positioning the cursor and pointing with it than can ever be achieved with the four cursor (or arrow) keys of the standard keyboard. The mouse really comes into its own as an input device in a WIMP (Windows Icon Mouse and Pull-down menus) environment within which most commands can be invoked by pointing the cursor at small icons (symbols) on the screen rather than having to key in the required command letter by letter. Systems offering such environments are currently more common (in percentage terms) with Apple machines than IBM clones, but as has been stressed earlier it is these latter which dominate most management applications. The mouse and the keyboard can also be complementary to each other

A mouse will be supplied with its own specialized software which must be installed before the mouse can be used. Quite often this software will have to be configured for the particular applications package with which it is intended to use the mouse.

10.3 Touchscreen

The reasoning behind the touch-sensitive screen is the same 'see and point' philosophy as that behind the mouse. Instructions are given to the computer by pointing at various icons on the screen. The difference is that this time the pointing is done directly by your own finger; you actually touch not the screen itself, but a grid of fine wires in front of the screen, so that the computer can work out where your finger is pressing. The touchscreen has the advantage of being a very natural way to do things, since it is just like pressing a button. However, it is not as accurate as pointing with a mouse and cursor. Touchscreen applications are therefore most successful where only a very limited amount of input is required. One example is in computer or video demonstrations at exhibitions, where the viewer/user chooses which part to see next by touching the appropriate rectangle on the screen, and can also enter data from a pre-determined set of choices. For example, a health education demonstration may ask for your sex, age, whether you smoke or not, and so on. Hewlett-Packard has been one of the most active vendors of touchscreen systems.

10.4 Voice

This type of input covers an extremely wide range of applications of varying degrees of sophistication. The most widespread are systems designed to deal with telephone enquiries. The use of voice input is a natural step up from the use of a touch-tone telephone which is how these systems began. These voice response systems actually have a very limited understanding of spoken English — for example, just the digits from zero to nine and the words yes and no. That's why the term 'voice input' is really a more accurate one than 'speech input', at least at present. The human–computer interaction is structured so that these are the only responses which the human needs to make, and so are the only ones the computer has to deal with. These systems are often combined with voice output, in the form of pre-recorded words or phrases.

At a higher level of sophistication are voice input systems designed to control an ordinary personal computer. These systems are normally user-dependent, i.e. designed for a specific user, whereas the telephone answering systems are user independent, i.e. designed for anyone to use. The user-dependent systems have a much greater 'vocabulary' than the user-independent ones, but they have to be 'trained'. The user has to speak all the key words which the system is required to know a number of times (usually at least three) until the system has detected enough of a pattern in the different examples of the same word to recognize it again. Systems which can recognize several hundred words are available, but tend to be of value only in certain situations, for example with disabled users, or where hands-off operation of the system is required, for example in a manufacturing plant where employees typically have wet or dirty hands.

True speech input, i.e. of continuous spoken sentences rather than individual words, is a subject of great research interest at present, but has not quite become commercially feasible yet. (See also the Artificial Intelligence section 3.16.)

10.5 Pen

Until very recently, pen input meant the so-called light pen. This is basically a pen-shaped torch. The functions of the light pen are the same as those of the mouse and the touchscreen; it is as accurate as the former (the point of the light pen being much narrower than that of your finger) but, like the latter, requires special technology as well as the normal screen. Thus, like the mouse, it was originally used in graphics applications. The mouse seemed to have won the battle against the pen as the 1990s began, but there has now been a new development. Pen input now refers most commonly not to a light pen, but to a combination of a solid *stylus* (pen) and a sensitive *tablet* (to write on). Because it relies on pressure rather than on light, this makes it feasible for the computer, with the aid of appropriate software, to accept handwritten input. As with voice input, you do have to 'train' it to recognize your handwriting first, though. The pen/stylus can also be used for the same functions that a touchscreen performs. Pen input is a particularly attractive option to personal computer manufacturers because of the trend towards ever smaller machines. There is a limit to how small a typewriter-style keyboard can be made and still remain useful, and present machines are going below that limit, especially those which have recently been named personal digital assistants (PDAs). You've probably discovered that it's almost impossible to use more than two fingers to press the keys on a pocket calculator, and the same problem afflicts manufacturers who are trying hard to produce a true pocket computer. Since the tablet can be made much smaller than a keyboard, the manufacturers hope that it will catch on with users. Pen input is not intended to replace the keyboard in keyboard-intensive applications like word-processing, but it is quite possible that it will suffice for the applications used on PDAs such as diaries and address books. Whether it will or not will no doubt become clear in the next year or two.

10.6 Other input devices

The *tracker ball* works on a similar principle to the mouse, but is built-in to the keyboard, or plugged into the side of it, and so does not require the extra desk space. This is particularly important for portable computers, where there may not be a desk to put the mouse on. The *joystick* actually accomplishes similar functions as well, although its design reflects its association with games use; we are not aware of any business computing applications specifically designed to accept joystick input, though it would certainly be possible to use it in that way.

Moving to more automated methods, *bar codes* are probably familiar to everyone, as they appear on more and more types of product. They are so common that the production of different types of bar code reader is a specialized market in itself; we won't go into the details here. Bar code readers in shops identify each product swiftly and accurately, and enable the shop to work out how much to charge the customer by reference to a price database on their computer. Note that when this was originally introduced in the UK, some troubles arose because of the prices file being changed (upwards, of course) between the time the customer picked the product off the shelf and the time when they reached the check-out. Legislation on price marking has had to be modified to prevent this practice. Bar codes are also in common use for such diverse purposes as stock control and recording the finishers in marathon races.

Optical character recognition, or OCR, is the answer — in most cases, at least — to the question of how to input existing printed documents into a computer system without re-typing them. Originally OCR only worked with special *fonts* which were easy for the system to read, so you had to know in advance that you were likely to want to put the document concerned into a computer system, or it would not work! Current OCR systems will recognize most standard typewriter and printer fonts, and are correspondingly much more useful. Advertisements usually quote figures of '99% accuracy', which sounds fine until you realize that this means one word wrong in every hundred, when a typical printed page contains anything from 250 to 500 words. OCR systems thus do still need human intervention.

Optical mark recognition is one of the simplest input systems, but very effective. You may have experienced this if you have taken an automatically-marked multiple-choice test; usually, a soft pencil is used to fill in a box or circle corresponding to the answer for each question, and all the system does is to 'read the blobs'. The same technology is also used to input questionnaire responses for computer analysis, and a slightly more sophisticated version of the same principle is used by the football pools companies such as Littlewoods and Vernons, to read in the entries from each football coupon.

Finally, to mention a very special-purpose input system which has been around for years and is still performing sterling service, *magnetic ink* was at the basis of computerizing the banking system. The slightly odd-looking numbers along the bottom of your cheques and paying-in slips giving branch and account details were printed with special magnetic ink. This enabled them to be 'read by machine', i.e. directly input to the banks' computer systems, in the days long before OCR had been invented.

This is not intended to be a complete list; we have not mentioned direct logging of data into the computer, used in all kinds of process control and experiments, or the data glove, currently associated with virtual reality games (see section 3.15), or modems (see section 14). However, we have tried to be quite comprehensive, to give an idea of the range of alternatives to the keyboard which is available.

11 | Processor

The processor is the 'brain' of the computer; the part which does the actual computing. The term brain is really a misnomer, as its functionality bears little resemblance to that of human or animal brains. *The phrase 'electronic brain' was in fact coined for the Univac computer which successfully predicted (live on television) the outcome of the 1952 US Presidential election on the basis of the early results. Unfortunately, as the prediction was at odds with what the opinion pollsters had been expecting, the TV presenter didn't believe the output, and so didn't announce it to the viewing millions! The true prediction was only revealed to the public after the actual result was known.*

Modern personal computers may have not just a single processor, but two (the second one is typically one which is faster than the normal one at carrying out complex mathematical operations, and takes over when needed). However, even if it does have two processors, the typical personal computer (and indeed most larger machines also) effectively works as if it has only one, i.e. it can only do one thing at a time. This design is called the Von Neumann architecture, after the designer of one of the earliest computers. Computers with more than two processors may also be designed in this manner, but more normally this brings us into the realms of true *parallel processing,* in which different processors work on different tasks (or different parts of the same task) at the same time. True parallel processing machines are at present only used in scientific and military operations such as image (picture) recognition; further discussion is therefore beyond the scope of this book.

The processors in all modern computers, whether microcomputers or not, are actually microprocessors. Don't let this confuse you; it's simply that the reduction in size of processors generally to the level at which the term microprocessor was coined made the microcomputer possible. The discussion here concentrates on microcomputers, as this is where more fuss is made about the processor than in other segments of the hardware market. As we said in the introduction, ideally you (the user) should be worrying about the software, not the hardware, but it is difficult to remember this when faced with current personal computer magazines.

11.1 Personal 'IBM compatible' microcomputing hardware

In the late 1970s, the development of early microcomputer processor chips allowed enthusiasts to buy kits of parts and assemble simple computers. This 'hobbyist' market, based mainly in the USA, spawned a series of relatively small companies who started designing and building microcomputers for sale as complete, ready-to-use units such that by the early 1980s microcomputers sold by companies such as Apple, Commodore and Tandy were generally available in the marketplace but were not really powerful enough to tackle real business tasks.

More importantly however, these machines were unable to exchange information with each other since, at that time, it was thought to be in the commercial interest of the companies involved to restrict users only to their machines through unique operating systems and unique disk formats.

During 1981–82 this position began to change with the introduction of a disk-based operating system named CP/M, which rapidly became an accepted standard, together with an increase in internal memory size to 64 Kbytes. At the same time, the increasing degree of uniformity in disk formats allowed for the exchange of information via floppy disks between microcomputers of different manufacturers.

It was, however, the introduction of the IBM PC (Personal Computer) to the UK in 1983 which completely changed the microcomputer marketplace from one of non-standardization and inadequate power to a situation where PCs with their distributed power and *user friendly* software began to compete with the then mini- and main-frame machines.

The IBM PC represented IBM's first move into microcomputers and, although not technically the most advanced machine of its day, it established what every other microcomputer manufacturer accepted as the 'standard' with which they had to compete. The early IBM PC based on the Intel 8088 processor chip came with

- a standard 256 Kbytes of internal memory (RAM - Random Access Memory),

- twin 360 Kbyte floppy, 5.25 inch disk drives (external memory), and

- an operating system named PC/MS-DOS.

The IBM (PC) offered a standard which encouraged end-users to believe that at long last a microcomputer had been developed which was powerful enough in terms of both processing power and storage capacity to perform real tasks and was standard enough to allow for exchange of information between machines produced by different manufacturers. Another important aspect of standardization, particularly in terms of the operating system provided to run the IBM PC, namely Microsoft's PC/MS-DOS, was that it would allow software (i.e. program) developers to produce applications packages which, with such a large potential market, allowed development costs to be recouped with packages priced at well below £500. This represented about 20–30% of the then hardware cost (i.e. the cost of the physical bits and pieces which made up the standard microcomputer).

Today (in the early 90s), as a result of technical progress, particularly with the development of hard disks, the price drop of storage chips and competition between manufacturers, a typical *entry level* PC would have;

- 2 – 4 Mbytes of internal memory or RAM (8 to 16 times the size of that available on the original IBM PC), together with

- a hard disk of 80 Mbytes (100 times the size of the twin floppy disks of the original IBM PC).

11.2 The processor chip

The speed and power of a microcomputer depend primarily on the type of processor chip around which the computer is designed. The majority (something like 85% of the UK market) of business microcomputers developed from the original IBM PC and are based on a family of processor chips developed originally by Intel, the only significant competitor being the Apple range of machines which are based on Motorola chips.

The original IBM PC used the Intel 8088 processor chip. The main advantage of this chip compared with its predecessors was that as a 16-bit processor chip it was capable of addressing more internal memory than the 64 Kbytes limit of the early 8- bit chip machines.

However, the subsequent development of 16/32-bit processors has removed the technical limitation of memory addressability such that internal memory size is now limited either by cost or technical reasons other than addressability.

The introduction of the IBM PC based on the 8088 Intel chip introduced a standard for personal microcomputers which IBM's many competitors used as the basis for their machines which therefore became known as 'clones', 'look-alikes', 'compatibles' etc. and which attempted to offer:

- faster operating speeds

- cheaper prices for the same facilities

- bundled (i.e. free) software

- more storage at the same price.

The family of *PC compatibles* based on the Intel 8088 processor chip peaked in 1987 with world-wide sales of 4.5 million and still currently represents a massive existing installed base of machines. However, because of their relatively slow speed of operation and, by today's standards, limited memory this **PC** family of machines is now very dated although for those users who have a single requirement, such as word-processing, still offer a cheap and reliable solution.

The successor to the 8088 chip was the 8086, a true 16-bit processor chip which offered higher operating speeds and proportionally more memory addressability. This chip, used as the basis for the IBM XT microcomputer, spawned the **XT** family of machines which also incorporated as standard a hard disk, as opposed to the early twin floppy configuration of the PCs. This increased the external memory capacity from 2×360 Kbytes to a single 360 Kbyte floppy disk plus a 10 Mbyte hard disk — a fifteen-fold increase.

Inevitably, with improving processor chip design, the **XT** family of machines in its turn was succeeded by a new family of microcomputers based on the Intel 80286 chip which was brought to the marketplace as the IBM AT (Advanced Technology) machine. With more speed and power than the earlier **PC** or **XT** micros, sales of the **AT** family of machines peaked in 1989 at 4.5 millions.

The **PC**, **XT** and **AT** families of microcomputers all represented improving developments of single-user microcomputers based broadly on improving processor chip technology but without changing the basic overall concept and design.

However, with the introduction in 1987 of the range of PS/2 models based on the Intel 80386 32-bit processor chip, IBM broke from the traditional mould of model improvement by moving to both a different (3.5 inch) floppy disk format and a fundamental change of internal design based on Micro Channel Architecture (MCA). This latter was introduced partly to make it more difficult for 'clone makers' to copy and also to allow for easier integration with traditional mainframe computer architecture. The IBM PS/2 range of machines covered a wide spectrum of computing power and storage facilities with the PS/2 Model 30 at the bottom of the range and the PS/2 Model 60 towards the top end of the range with enough power to make the definition of the boundary between what could be defined as a microcomputer (usually assumed to be a single-user machine) and a minicomputer (usually assumed to be a multiple-user machine) very blurred. Sales of the PS/2 family of machines peaked at 7 million world-wide in 1991.

Although, in 1993, PCs being sold based on the 80386 Intel chip design (or one of its variants) still represented a significant proportion of the market, already the next generation of chips, heralded by the 80486, was appearing in faster and more powerful machines at the top end of the market, at only marginally higher prices.

Even newer chips are now being demonstrated, with still better performance, including the latest from Intel, which is called the Pentium rather than the 80586 because names may be protected by trade mark legislation but numbers may not! Rivals to the Pentium also set to appear in personal computers include the Alpha and PowerPC chips.

The original development of the IBM PC and the many variants that followed it has had a dramatic influence on the development of personal computers which in turn has led to a move away from mini- and main-frame systems to networks of PCs operating with *distributed power,* i.e. each machine has power to perform its own processing rather than sharing processing power held centrally. Although IBM's power and influence has been challenged by a whole host of competitors, this company is still a major player in the market, as the sales figures in the UK for the year to March 1993 shown in Table 12 demonstrate.

Table 12 Personal computer hardware sales in the UK (year to March 1993)

	By volume	By value
Compaq	21.4%	21.6%
IBM	20.0%	20.9%
Apple	12.1%	12.6%
Toshiba	6.9%	11.9%
Tandon	3.9%	3.6%
Olivetti	3.7%	2.2%
Amstrad	2.9%	1.4%
Apricot	2.8%	2.5%
ICL	2.7%	3.1%

No other company has a market share of 2% or more, either by volume or by value.

Note that these figures exclude the Amstrad PCW series from the market entirely. Including it would increase Amstrad's market shares to 4.8% by volume and 1.8% by value, with a corresponding decrease in the shares of other companies.

Source: *Computing*/Context.

All the microcomputer systems considered so far have been the conventional *desk-top* type of machine with, as separate but connected units:

● The microcomputer's main processor unit containing all the elements required to define a standard micro, with the exception of

● The VDU (Visual Display Unit, see section 12 for more details) and

● The keyboard (see section 10 for more details)

Two other microcomputer system configurations that have to be considered in addition to the standard desk-top system are the portable and laptop microcomputers.

Portable and laptop microcomputers normally weigh between 12 lbs and 18 lbs and incorporate in one unit the microcomputer processor, screen and keyboard. These machines are obviously aimed at that market sector which places a premium on portability. Although similar in appearance, the essential difference between the two is that the portable requires a mains voltage electricity supply whereas the laptop can run off either a mains supply or a built-in battery.

In practice the source of electricity supply controls the type of screen that can be used. The mains-powered portable generally uses a high-voltage gas plasma technology whereas the laptop uses a low-voltage liquid crystal display (LCD) technology similar to that used in battery-powered calculators. The gas plasma screen is regarded as producing a better definition than LCD screens and is less sensitive to light reflection. However, LCD screen technology has improved to such an extent that this market sector, in which true portability is required, has extended significantly in recent years.

11.3 Larger machines

One of the keys to the successful marketing of larger machines in recent years has been *modularity*; offering a range of machines with interchangeable components (processors, terminals, storage devices) which can be configured to the client's requirements. Digital (DEC) achieved much of its success during the 1980s on this basis, with its VAX range of mini- and main-frame computers, and the aid of the XCON expert system (see section 3.11). Naturally this move has been emulated by others, for example IBM with its AS/400 series. Most machines can be *clustered*, so that several separate processors appear to the user as if they were one system. These are the machines with several microprocessors which follow the Von Neumann sequential architecture, as we mentioned earlier.

As with personal computers, there has been a good deal to be gained in the mainframe computer market by following the lead of IBM. This is the so-called plug-compatible market, where a company such as Amdahl manufactures equipment such as processors which is designed to function with IBM peripherals (terminals, storage devices, etc.).

One of the more recent developments in larger machines has been the move towards what is called RISC (reduced instruction set computing) architecture. These systems are based on microprocessors whose machine code contains fewer instructions than the previous generation of microprocessors' machine code did, thus reversing a trend over many years for the number of instructions to increase. The extra speed of the processor chip itself more than compensates for the fact that a program written in a high-level language compiles into more instructions on a RISC machine than it did previously.

12 | Output devices

As with input devices, output devices are either for output to human beings, or to other computers. This section concentrates on output in a form suitable for humans, the other being covered in the section on communications. The most suitable form of output for humans is something we can look at (words and/or pictures); people are used to receiving output from other people in the form of words and pictures, and most output devices work in this manner. Originally this meant the computer producing paper tape or punched cards which another machine could 'translate' into printed output, but later these functions (for words, but not pictures) were combined with that of the teletype, a kind of automatic typewriter which could be used for both input and output. This made genuinely interactive systems possible, and the subsequent invention of the Visual Display Unit and the line printer produced vast improvements in the speed of producing readable and hard copy output respectively.

The visual display unit is in a technological sense the most important output device, because without at least one visual display unit a modern computer, especially a personal computer, cannot sensibly be operated. However, even for personal computers the printer runs it close in terms of importance, and for many large business computer systems the sheer volume of printed output (invoices, cheques, bank statements) makes the printer the most important output device in business terms. In this section we discuss the visual display unit, printers and (rather more briefly) plotters and voice output.

12.1 Visual display unit (VDU)

The VDU is the part of the computer that looks like a television screen. There are slight differences between the two technologies, but they need not concern us here. Indeed, many early home microcomputers used a television screen as the main output device.

The quality of any computer screen display is a function of the number of pixels (the individual dot or smallest addressable element) that make up the screen display and is, therefore, a function of the amount of internal memory dedicated to that purpose; usually mounted on a special board or card within the computer.

In ascending order of cost the various forms of screen display are:

● Mono (standard resolution of 200×320 pixels)

- Mono (Hercules - resolution of 200×640 pixels)

- Colour (CGA - Colour Graphics Adaptor - capable of displaying 16 colours at a resolution of 200×350 pixels)

- Colour (EGA - Enhanced Graphics Adaptor - capable of displaying 16 colours at a resolution of 640×350 pixels)

- Colour (VGA - Video Graphics Array - capable of displaying 256 colours at a resolution of 640×480 pixels and requiring 256 kbytes of RAM)

- Colour (SVGA - Super Video Graphics Array - capable of displaying 256 colours at a resolution of 1044×760 pixels and requiring at least 512 kbytes of RAM).

It is difficult to compare these precisely with the quality of a television picture, because it is made up in a slightly different way. It is probably fair to say that a normal television is slightly better than VGA, but not as good as SVGA.

12.2 Printers

There are currently several different technologies involved in translating computer output into printed copy (i.e. hard copy) offering differing purchase and running costs, print speeds, print quality and operating noise levels.

Traditionally impact dot-matrix technology has dominated the microcomputing scene but the improved reliability of ink-jet technology, in particular, has seen a recent surge in sales of this type of printer for personal computing. Also, with cost reductions in laser printing technology, although still perhaps a little too expensive for a single user, simple networking permits several users to economically share a laser printer and thus achieve a higher level of print quality.

In terms of paper handling, originally most printers were designed to cope with continuous stationery using a *tractor feed* mechanism. Improving reliability of cut-sheet feeders, which cope with individual pages, has now led an increasing proportion of the market to opt for this type of paper handling. Traditionally a cut-sheet feeder was an optional extra to a standard printer with a tractor feed, but many machines are now coming onto the market aimed at the personal user which only offer individual page handling, typically for A4 sized paper.

Standard printers offer a page width of 80 characters. (*This goes back to the days of punched cards again; each card could contain 80 characters!*) Wider page widths are coped with either by machines fitted with a wider than normal carriage offering a page width of 120 or 132 characters, or by using *compressed* printing; 120 characters per line can be printed using a printer with a normal 80 character width carriage.

Dot-matrix printers

The dot-matrix printer uses a technology based on a print head made up either of a single row of 8 or 9 pins or, more recently, of a double row made up of 18, 24 or even 48 pins. The positioning of individual pins in either the *print* or *recessed* position is controlled by the computer and each printed character is, therefore, formed as a series of dots. These dots are transferred to paper via a traditional carbon ribbon by the impacting of the ribbon between pins and paper. Obviously the more dots used to represent a character the better the definition, hence 18/24/48-pin printers produce better quality print than 8/9-pin printers.

Print quality can be improved by increasing the number of *passes* made along the line being printed but this obviously reduces overall printing speeds. The current maximum printing speed for this type of technology is about 400 cps (characters per second). For reasonable print quality the dot-matrix printer is fast, noisy and well established. Where multiple stationery sets are used, for example to produce an invoice/delivery note set, dot-matrix technology does provide the necessary physical impact to produce multiple copies which is not the case with ink-jet and laser printers.

Ink-jet printers

Ink-jet printer technology has been around for some time but only since 1988 have printers based on the ink-jet concept really become a commercial proposition. Ink-jet printers use differing methods to project droplets of ink from microscopic nozzles directly on to paper. In the past there have been problems of nozzles becoming blocked, ink not being suitable for normal paper and general unreliability. These technical problems have now been successfully overcome and ink-jet printers are now increasing their market share considerably with a quality of print similar to laser printers, i.e. 300 dpi (dots per inch) and virtually total quietness in operation.

Another advantage of ink-jet printers is that they can print directly onto the acetate sheets used in conjunction with overhead projectors for formal presentations. Colour ink-jet printers are also available, and are bound to become more popular as colour copying becomes more common. However, one slight disadvantage of ink-jet printers is that the image smudges when wet — so be careful when posting letters in the rain!

Laser printers

Laser printers are based on a similar technology to Xerography, the copying process used in most photocopiers. However, whereas in photocopying the image to be copied is transferred by a fluorescent light source to an electrostatically charged, rotating cylinder directly from the original hard copy master; in a laser printer the image is 'written' on the cylinder using a laser light beam controlled by the microcomputer. Once the electrostatic copy of the image to be printed is available, the production of hard copy by a process of transferring this image by attracting coloured resin onto sensitized paper is essentially the same in both devices.

Laser printers are still relatively more expensive than other printing technologies, particularly in terms of running costs. They produce a very high quality of print (300 dpi or better) and have increased their share of the printer market recently in line with the popularity of desk-top publishing. Many laser printers offer facilities for using specialized print fonts which are generated within a small microcomputer built into the printer.

More expensive, high volume laser printers offer simple networking facilities so that several users can make use of the same printer.

The current state of the printer market in the UK (Romtec figures for 1992) is that in terms of volume, i.e. number of units sold, dot-matrix, ink-jet and laser printers each have a roughly one-third share, with around 1% of sales still being the even older daisy-wheel technology (as used in some electric typewriters). However, in terms of sales *value*, the greater unit cost of laser printers pushes their share up to around 60%.

12.3 Plotters

Most printers can now print graphics of some kind, the exceptions being daisy-wheel printers and some of the cheapest of the dot-matrix variety, which are still character-based. In the days when virtually all printers were character-based, then producing graphical output required a plotter — a device specifically intended for producing graphs, charts, etc. The original plotters literally had pens which drew the images on the paper. The technology has improved since then, and there is still a market for plotters wherever there is a requirement for specialized graphics work. This is particularly true where large diagrams are required, as in engineering and architecture, and so plotters are often found as part of computer-aided design systems. They are also often used with project management packages, for similar reasons.

12.4 Voice output

Voice output is a considerably easier problem to deal with than voice input. The digital audio revolution has made it possible to store spoken words in ordinary computer memory, which may be selectively retrieved by direct (i.e. random) access. The sounds take up quite a lot of space in the memory, especially for a good representation of a human voice rather than one which sounds like a Dalek, and so these work best with a limited vocabulary. If you telephone British Telecom's directory enquiries, after a human operator has found the correct entry in BT's database, you will hear the number you require 'spoken' by a voice output system.

13 | Memory/storage

Computers operate essentially with two types of memory, namely internal memory (in the form of memory chips) and external memory (usually, for microcomputers, in the form of floppy or hard disks). Relatively speaking, internal memory is fast but volatile, i.e. when the computer is switched off such memory loses its stored information. External memory is relatively slow but, accidents apart, permanent.

Internal memory

A computer's internal memory is usually in the form of Random Access Memory (RAM) chips. Because this form of memory is fast, the more that is available the faster any particular task can be executed. For most PCs the current minimum standard for internal memory for operating in a PC/MS-DOS environment is 640 Kbytes, which has to store:

- The operating system, i.e. the programs that run the computer and are required irrespective of the application involved

- Information supporting screen displays; the better the screen definition, the more memory required

- The most commonly used elements of the application package

- Data (both textual and numerical) for the particular application being processed

In today's PC market, the more powerful microcomputers in the PS/2 range and their 80386/80486 equivalents are now available with several Megabytes of internal memory which are indeed a prerequisite for operating many of today's software packages, particularly if those packages operate in a Windows environment.

External memory

Because internal memory only stores information while the computer is switched on, all information which it is necessary to retain on a permanent basis must be held in external memory — usually in the form of floppy or hard disks for personal computers, and hard disks, disk packs or tapes for larger systems.

Currently the position on the various forms of magnetic disk storage can be summarized as shown in Table 13.

Table 13 Types of microcomputer magnetic disk, size and capacity

Type of disk	Size	Capacity
Standard floppy	5.25 inch	360 Kbytes to 1.6 Mbytes
Micro floppy	3.5 inch	720 Kbytes to 1.44 Mbytes
Hard disk	various	10 Mbytes to 200 Mbytes

Floppy disks only rotate when information is either being read from them or written to them and, hence, are relatively slow devices compared with hard disks. However, floppy disks can be removed from the microcomputer and are, therefore, a suitable medium for permanent storage of backup information.

Hard disks rotate from the moment the computer is switched on and spin at much higher speeds than floppy disks and, therefore, are much faster devices in terms of read and write access times. The speed of a hard disk is usually expressed in terms as an average *seek* time which is typically in the range from 10 to 20 milliseconds (thousandths of a second). Larger computers use a similar technology to the hard disks, but with even greater capacity (as high as 2 *Giga*bytes, or 2000 Mbytes) and even shorter access times (less than 10 milliseconds). This is usually achieved by having storage systems containing multiple disks which operate as a set.

As in the music industry, optical storage media are beginning to challenge magnetic media as devices for external memory/storage. A particular impetus for this has been the expansion in the use of graphics, which drastically increases memory/storage requirements. For example, a typical A4 page of text, stored as characters, occupies about 5 Kbytes of memory. Store the same page as graphics, and it might take up more than 1 Mbyte (200 times as much), depending on the format used and the resolution. A full-colour photograph the same size might take as much as 60 Mbytes, although there are compression techniques available which reduce this by an order of magnitude.

The much greater capacity of devices based on optical disks is therefore sorely needed for some applications: the most common is the CD-ROM (Compact Disk - Read Only Memory), using a virtually identical technology to that on music CDs. This typically gives a capacity of 660 Mbytes, with a seek time of 320 milliseconds.(Compare these figures with those for hard disks mentioned earlier.) Other types of optical disk offer slightly greater capacities, but the widespread use of CD-ROM technology gives it a marketplace advantage.

All external computer disk storage is vulnerable to loss of information. Although the reliability of such devices is now much better than it was, crashes (losses of information) do happen and it is always sensible to have a formalized 'backing-up' (copying) procedure which ensures that if problems do arise the system can be resurrected without too much effort (see section 9). For the *personal* microcomputer user, floppy disks offer the most convenient back-up medium. However, where large amounts of data are to be retained by *corporate* or *power* users, specialized magnetic tape storage systems (often referred to as *tape streamers*) are more appropriate. Again, the optical storage devices are also beginning to be used for back-up purposes, because of their large capacity. On mini-computers and mainframes, one of the latest technological advances is the so-called *raid* (redundant arrays of independent disks) storage device, which uses techniques ranging from *mirroring* (keeping two copies on different disks) to *striping* each file across several disks. This provides storage facilities which can cope with the loss of at least one of the disks without loss of data.

The latest generation of palm-top computers or personal digital assistants are too small to accommodate conventional disk drives. This has been one of the reasons for the development of the credit card-sized memory cards produced to the PCMCIA (Personal Computer Memory Card International Association) standard. Prices are very high compared to other types of storage, and most cards sold at present are 128Kbytes or 256Kbytes in size. However, there is already a card on the market with a capacity of 105Mbytes, and if prices come down sufficiently they may begin to challenge conventional disk drives in the desktop personal computer market. At present the only PCMCIA slots on conventional PCs are intended for transfer of information from smaller machines.

14 | Communications

Many people in computing see the revolution which occurred in the late 1980s in networking, or to be more precise, data communications, as one of the major advances in information technology. To be pedantic, whenever two or more pieces of computer hardware (such as a terminal and a mainframe processor, or a personal computer and a printer) need to be connected together, data communications issues arise. As you can imagine, this applies to the vast majority of situations in which computers are used. However, the word network is normally used to refer to situations where the connections involve two or more computers. At its simplest, this could be two personal computers such as PCs or Apple Macintoshes sharing a resource such as a laser printer. At the other extreme, it could be a company's world-wide corporate information network involving thousands of computers in a hundred different countries. The line defining a network is usually drawn just 'above' the bottom end of this scale, so that as soon as the link is actually between two or more computers, to allow data to be exchanged or shared between them, then it counts as a network. Networks are discussed in more detail in the section which follows this one.

Despite this recent explosion of interest, the idea of communication between computers is probably at least as old as that of the electronic computer itself. In a limited sense, it has been possible in practice ever since the invention of the punched card and the paper tape made it possible to store programs outside the computer itself, although this was only guaranteed to work between two computers of the same type running the same operating system. Electronic communication between computers is not only faster and more efficient, but offers the possibility of connecting computers of different types and using different operating systems. The latter is often a harder problem than the former; this was one of the reasons behind the development of the Unix operating system (see section 1.4). Technology has now progressed to the extent where it is now possible to connect virtually any two computers together (although it remains easier for some combinations than for others!).

Initially the main uses of communications were within organizations: for data transfer, back-up and applications such as electronic mail (see section 3.6). These often required little extra connectivity than was already in place. Connecting terminals and other peripherals to a mainframe or mini-computer based system is actually a communications issue also, as we have said; all that was required in addition were connections *between* computers. Thus, in the pre-personal computer era, taking care of communications at this level remained solely the province of those responsible for running the computers anyway.

However, as computers moved into the home and onto the desktop, and communications facilities improved, more exciting possibilities arose, broadly in three directions.

(i) If a local computer on a manager's desktop could communicate with other computers in the organization, then the company's computing requirements could be distributed between the local computers (those on the desktop) and the central ones.

(ii) Organizations could communicate and exchange data with each other electronically, instead of having to rely on paper.

(iii) Home computer users could communicate and exchange data with each other electronically, instead of having to rely on exchanging disks.

A fourth direction, really combining (ii) and (iii), is that business users with a computer at home could exchange data between their home computer and their computer at work.

Perhaps the key development for the computer user at home was the invention of a device called the modem, which stands for modulator/demodulator, to enable a microcomputer to communicate with other computers over telephone lines. In order to do this, the bits (0s and 1s) of the computer data have to be converted into audible tones (by a process known as modulation) which can be transmitted over the telephone system in much the same way as normal speech. When such audible signals are received they also need to be reconverted into the 0s and 1s that the computer can process (i.e. demodulation). Thus a modem (or equivalent) is needed at both the sending and receiving computers. Modems operate at different speeds which are required to match the capabilities of the types of computer involved, the communications software they are using, and the type of line being used to link them. These speeds are measured in baud rates; there are actually two slightly different definitions of baud rate, but the most common is the number of bits transmitted per second. Typical rates vary from 300 baud up to 9600 baud. The *de facto* industry standard for modems is the Hayes protocol.

At a rate of 1200 baud, a single-page document would take around half a minute to transmit, which demonstrates that modems are not really fast enough for large-scale business use. Nevertheless, a modem is still quite satisfactory for some business uses, for example where only small amounts of information need to be transmitted at one time, such as in electronic mail, or where the transmission may be done at night, so that speed is less important. Whatever its limitations, many home computer users in particular have found that the use of a modem has enabled them to become part of a much wider 'computer community'.

For high-speed (and high volume) data communications, the ordinary analogue telephone lines need to be replaced by special digital lines, designed for data, rather than sound, transmission. A company may either install its own (an expensive business) or lease lines from a telecommunications company. A strange quirk of this split between the analogue (sound) and digital worlds is that the performance of the digital lines is actually described in different terms: bits per second, rather than baud rate, although it amounts to the same thing! In the UK, British Telecom offers its Kilostream and Megastream digital leased lines operating at 64 Kbits per second and 2 Mbits per second respectively. This makes the Kilostream lines over 50 times faster than a 1200 baud modem, and the Megastream lines more than 30 times faster still. In fact, the capacity of the fastest lines is often used for simultaneous transmission of many 'channels' of information, rather than just one.

The principles and uses of this technology, especially in directions (i) and (ii) above, are described further in the following two sections: on networks and networking, and electronic data interchange.

14.1 Networks and networking

In the previous section on Communications, we defined a network as referring to any system enabling data communications between two or more computers. Looking at network systems in business, we find there are three modes of use, although these are by no means mutually exclusive. The first is the linking of individual computers together, to permit the sharing of data and programs, and also the use of such applications as personal computer-based electronic mail systems. Note that this was needed to give personal computer users the same sharing of data and applications that users of terminal-based systems had taken for granted for years. The second mode of use is on a somewhat broader scale within the organization, to allow *downloading* of data from mainframe or mini-computer into the personal productivity tools on a manager's desktop machine such as spreadsheets, word-processors and databases. This ensures that all computer users have access to up-to-date information about the organization without the bother of having to maintain it themselves. Note that technically it is equally possible to *upload* data from the personal computer to the mainframe, but security reasons make this a very different process from the management point of view, and certainly not one which can be allowed to go uncontrolled (see section 9). Nevertheless, there are many occasions when this will be done, for example by sales staff in the field recording orders during the day on a portable computer, for transmission to the organization's main computer(s) via a modem during the night; the confectionery firm Rowntree Mackintosh were one of the first in the UK to do this. The third mode of use is to facilitate *downsizing* — replacing a big machine by a number of smaller machines in order to reduce capital and running costs. This is one of the 'hot topics' in business computing at present, with considerable debate about the extent to which this really does reduce total costs — if indeed it does reduce them at all! (See section 4 on Money.)

The most commonly-used acronym in networking is LAN, which stands for Local Area Network. This normally connects a number of personal computers, either in the same room (say a large general office or a student computer workshop) or in a set of physically adjacent rooms. All local area networks need three elements:

- Physical connections between the computers involved

- Special hardware, usually in the form of an extra plug-in card, which allows that machine to transmit and receive signals over the network (some personal computers already have this built-in)

- Software to control the transmission of signals over the network.

Where the networking software resides depends on which of two different types of local area network is in use: in a *peer-to-peer* network, each computer does a share of the work; whereas in a *server-based* network, one computer called the *file server* does most of the work, although some software is still needed on every machine. A file server usually has a higher specification than the other personal computers on the network, with considerably more external memory for storing shared data and programs, and perhaps a more powerful processor as well. The advantage of a peer-to-peer network is that the overhead of operating the network is relatively small; this works best for the simplest tasks such as sharing a high-quality printer and basic electronic mail. Server-based networks obviously require an extra computer, but are much more suitable when the main purpose of the network is to access common data or programs. No individual is likely to want the responsibility for storing everyone else's data unless it is specifically their job, and a server-based system makes the position very much clearer. Normally a server-based system requires the creation of a post of 'network administrator', at least part-time. With such a system, the spreadsheet or database package can be on the file server rather than the local personal computer (the one on the manager's desk). This gives the flexibility of use of a personal computer for the manager/user together with most of the ease of operation and maintenance of a mainframe or mini-computer for the system operators.

Once a system has one file server, there is little technological difficulty in adding further servers, with an appropriate division of 'responsibilities' between them. For this reason the downsizing, or decentralized, approach mentioned earlier is also often known as *client/server architecture,* the desktop personal computer being the client for the services offered by the various servers.

As in many other areas of computing, definitions are not entirely agreed, so it is not entirely clear when a LAN becomes a WAN or Wide Area Network (also called a broad area network). However, there is a definite limit on the distances over which LAN technology can work successfully. This limit is around 300 metres with the type of coaxial cabling which is most commonly used, but can be extended to about 1.5 kilometres by the use of appropriate boosters. Optical fibre connections give slightly better performance, but any distances longer than those on a fairly compact site require the use of the digital telecommunications technology mentioned in the previous section. A large organization, even on a single site, will probably have several LANs connected together by various bridges and routers. There are also hardware and software problems associated with controlling the 'traffic' on a network. The simplest method is to allow only one computer to transmit at any one time, which is fine for, say, a LAN with six users who only want to exchange occasional spreadsheet and word-processor files. However, it becomes more and more of a limitation as the number of computers and the amount of traffic increase; as a result, more sophisticated techniques are needed, typically involving equipment which is dedicated to running the network, further discussion of which is beyond the scope of this book — a suitable reference is Langley[1].

Network applications may also involve the use of the various public network systems available. Some of these offer connections: the JANET network connects UK universities together, and is itself connected to the Internet, which links universities and researchers in industry world-wide. As well as electronic mail, these networks permit file transfer and access to computer systems at other universities (although this may, of course, need the appropriate authorization). Connection to the Internet for commercial organizations is relatively expensive; companies such as Compuserve offer public network access, including electronic mail, at more affordable prices for smaller organizations or the self-employed. In addition to these networks, many organizations also provide data services, ranging from financial information such as share prices, to market research information. This kind of on-line access to data is a rapidly growing market at present.

Thus we have seen that networking large numbers of computers over long distances may bring both technological and management problems. A further complication is likely to arise from the appearance of software packages such as Lotus Notes, specifically intended to facilitate the work of a networked group of computer users. These take facilities such as shared data, diaries and electronic mail, and extend them fully into the context of tasks performed by a group. Meeting schedulers plan meetings on the basis of personal diaries; urgent electronic mail is automatically re-routed when the original recipient is unavailable; documents are forwarded to the next person who needs them ('workflow') and so on. As we speculated in the Introduction, this may prove to be a truly revolutionary development in business computing, but at the time of writing organizations are only beginning to come to grips with it.

The airline reservation systems accessed by travel agents have been perhaps the most visible example of network systems over the past few years, but there are many others. Indeed, the most pervasive are the networks in supermarkets and other large retail stores, where the electronic tills are linked to mini-computers for the up-to-the-minute exchange of price and stock control information. When these *electronic point of sale* (EPOS) systems are linked to others outside the organization, this takes us into the realms of electronic data interchange, as covered in the next section.

Reference
1. G.A. Langley and J.P. Ronayne *Telecommunications Primer* (fourth edition), Pitman, 1993.

14.2 Electronic data interchange

Electronic data interchange (EDI) is one of the latest technological advances towards the paperless office. It represents a convergence of two developments, one being the use of electronic mail, and the other the transfer of data within organizations by electronic means. In fact, most electronic mail is sent within organizations, or between people in different organizations with a common interest (such as organizing an academic conference); the use of electronic mail to pass messages *between* organizations for commercial purposes is relatively novel.

Most organizations, including virtually all of those involved in manufacturing and retailing, have commercial dealings with other organizations. Many of these interactions take place on standard printed forms such as purchase orders or invoices. Anything which is printed, and standardized, is a good candidate for production by computer (see sections 3.5 and 3.29), and this is commonly done already. However, the documents still have to be printed, and then physically sent to the recipient; this process takes time, and uses a lot of paper. It would be quicker, and perhaps better for the environment, if the information could be sent electronically. As well as this business-driven 'pull' in favour of EDI, there is also a technological 'push': given that organizations have information in electronic form, such as stock levels, and that there *are* electronic links to other organizations, it seems sensible to try to use them. For example, if the stock levels in a supermarket branch are automatically kept up-to-date from the electronic tills at the check-outs, it is straightforward for the computer in the branch to generate orders as and when necessary for replenishment from the supermarket's warehouse (probably checked by a member of the branch management first). This improves both the speed and the accuracy of the stock replenishment. Exactly the same logical operation is involved one step further back along the chain, at the warehouse itself: orders need to be generated based on actual stock levels and anticipated requirements. The only conceptual difference is that up to now everything has been within one organization (the supermarket chain); at this next stage many of the orders must now go to other organizations, i.e. the product suppliers.

The simplest way to achieve this communication is for the customer organization to have a terminal to the computer system of the supplier organization. This is essentially how the airline reservation systems mentioned in the previous section work. One or two other systems, especially in the financial services sector, also operate in this way. However, this structure is only feasible where a customer organization can deal exclusively with one supplier, and the service provided is crucial to the customer's successful operation. True EDI needs to be more general than this, and therefore must rely on a considerable amount of standardization. EDI systems, whether bought as packages off the shelf or written to order, therefore consist of a very structured form of messaging or electronic mail, to exchange the sort of data which would otherwise pass between organizations on printed forms, perhaps in confirmation of a previous telephone call. Note that although in theory the fax machine can replace the combination of letter and phone call, in practice most business dealings still involve confirming a fax message through the post; there appear to be lingering suspicions about the reliability of fax, not necessarily as a technology, but in terms of the message actually reaching the right person in the organization quickly enough.

The requirements for EDI systems are virtually the same as for networking: suitable hardware and software at each end, and suitable connections between the two computer systems. Technologically, there are thus no real difficulties. The harder problems are management ones: ensuring that *all* the relevant parties are connected up for EDI (or at least enough of them to form a 'critical mass' of users), and achieving the necessary changes in working practices. For example, the daily or weekly telephone call between regular customer and supplier may also provide the opportunity to exchange other useful information which an EDI system does not, even if EDI does remove the likelihood of errors in transmission. A further complication is that, in the UK at least, the legal status of an electronic order is questionable. Organizations undertaking EDI therefore often have to draw up an agreement beforehand setting out what they will regard as constituting evidence of a valid transaction, i.e. an *electronic signature*.

In spite of these management problems, EDI is catching on. Following on from the airline reservation example, it does still work best in situations either where each supplier has few customers (such as suppliers of components to the car industry), or where there are few competitors in the supplier's field (for example with British Steel). Retailing, with very many competing suppliers delivering to many competing customers, is therefore making slower progress with EDI for ordering. However, the electronic point-of-sale equipment in some shops is being used for a different form of EDI; the tills can be linked up with the banks' systems for authorization of credit card purchases, so that the enquiry for the amount of the transaction and the response (either a confirmation with an authorization number, or a rejection) are exchanged automatically.

Appendix 1
A guide to standard DOS facilities

A1.1 DOS filename descriptions

Because many DOS commands are concerned with files saved on disk, it would be sensible at this point to remind the reader that within DOS a complete description of a file consists of four elements namely;

- The optional disk drive specifier (or designation) which is defined with a single character followed by the full colon character (:). Hence a file on the **A** floppy disk drive would be prefixed with **A**: and a file on the hard-disk would generally be prefixed by **C**:

  The disk drive specifier is only optional in the sense that, if not specifically stated, DOS will assume the default disk drive, i.e. the drive preceding the \> prompt appearing on the screen.

- The **PATH**, which indicates in which directory and/or sub-directory the file is held. With the advent of hard disks it has clearly become necessary to sub-divide such large storage media into areas of more manageable size, but readers should be aware that directories and sub-directories can also usefully be created on floppy disks. A file's **PATH** is made up of the names of directories and sub-directories separated by the backslash character (\) which as the first character in a path represents the *root* directory, i.e. the highest directory. Hence a file held in a sub-directory **NORTH** of a directory **SALES** would be located by the path,

      \SALES\NORTH\

- The actual filename — which can consist of up to eight characters — should not contain spaces but can use the underline symbol (_) as a separator if necessary. A suitable name for the Wordstar file representing this appendix could, therefore, be **BCPAPP**. It pays to use some sensible logic when naming files if they are to be found with unerring accuracy six months later amongst the many others that will by then have been created.

- An extension consisting of three characters preceded by a full stop (.). The filename extension describes the type of file being referred to and is usually specified by the applications package. Hence in Lotus, spreadsheet files have the extension **.WK1** or **.WK3** and in dBASE III database files are given the extension **.DBF**. Text files produced by a word-processor could have an extension **.TXT** and backup files generally have the extension **.BAK**.

Summarizing the above, the full and complete description of a dBASE III database file **SALESREP** held on the **A** drive could be

    A:\SALESREP.DBF

whereas the same file held in the **NORTH** sub-directory of the **SALES** directory of the **C** drive could be;

    C:\SALES\NORTH\SALESREP.DBF

A1.2 Internal DOS commands

Internal DOS commands are always available when the DOS operating system has been loaded from the **COMMAND.COM** and associated files held on disk.

The internal DOS commands represent the more commonly used commands that the average personal user might require. The more important of these and their method of operation are described in the following section in alphabetical order.

Copying files between disks

(use of the **COPY** command)

For all sorts of reasons it is often necessary for a personal computer user to copy files from one disk to another. The DOS **COPY** command requires that both the source and name of the file or files to be copied and the destination or target disk to which they are to be copied be specified. For the inexperienced user it is recommended that source and destination drives are always specified in full, rather than the default drive being assumed.

The **COPY** command can be used in a variety of ways but in its basic form of copying a single file **SALESREP.DBF** from the **A** drive to **SALES** directory of **C** drive the command would be

    COPY A:\SALESREP.DBF C:\SALES

Using the so called *wild card* asterisk character (*), which can be used to represent any set of characters, it would be possible to copy all database files with the extension **.DBF** from the **A** drive to the **DBASE** directory of the **C** drive. The **COPY** command to achieve this would be

    COPY A:*.DBF C:\DBASE

With the proviso that enough space is available on the destination disk drive, to copy all files (irrespective of name or extension) from the **A** drive to the **MISC** directory of the **C** drive, the appropriate **COPY** command would be

COPY A\:*.* C:\MISC

The copy command can also be used to create simple text files without the necessity of loading a word-processor or text-editor. This can be very useful for creating small batch files (i.e. with the extension **.BAT**). To create a batch file on the **A** drive called **GO.BAT** containing the one dBASE command **DBASE MENU** would require the following

COPY CON: A:GO.BAT

DBASE MENU

^Z

where **^Z** is **CtrlZ**, that is the **Ctrl** key used in conjunction with the **Z** key.

Date and time setting

(use of the **DATE** and **TIME** commands)

Although most microcomputers now have built-in *clock-calendars* or *time-and-date clocks*, where it is important that the system date and time are changed, the **DATE** and **TIME** commands can be used to reset the current system settings. With regard to date, microcomputers without a clock-calendar generally return a system date of 01-01-1980. Most suppliers of personal computers in the UK do ensure that when initially configuring a microcomputer that the date format is that expected by Europeans, i.e. Date-Month-Year, as opposed to the North American Month-Date-Year format.

When the DOS commands **DATE** or **TIME** are keyed in, the current settings of the system date or time are displayed. If either needs changing, this is achieved by entering the new value using the same format as displayed.

All files saved in a DOS environment have the date and time of saving recorded. This is most useful in establishing which is the latest version of a file.

Directories of files

(use of the **DIR** command)

A list of filenames held on a disk is always maintained in the disk's directory. The **DIR** (directory) command can be used to indicate the names of files on a disk located in any specified disk drive.

The normal and most complete form of the **DIR** command for a disk located in the A drive would be

DIR A:

which then displays on the screen:

- the disk's volume name, if any

- the names of files held on the disk

- the size of files (in bytes)

- the date and time files were saved

- the number of files held, and

- the remaining disk space free (expressed in bytes).

An abbreviated form of the **DIR** command would be

DIR A:/w

which lists filenames horizontally (i.e. **w** = wide) to save space and also omits the sizes of files as well as the time and date when saved.

This abbreviated form of the **DIR** command is necessary if the user requires to see all file names on the screen when a large number of files are held on disk. If the user, however, wishes to see all the information provided by the normal **DIR** command but has too many files to be accommodated on the screen, the alternative command

DIR A:/p

displays a screen of filenames at a time and presents the next screen of filenames when any key is pressed (i.e. **p** = pause).

Erasing files from disks

(use of the **ERASE** command)

To create more space on a disk or to dispense with obsolete files, it is necessary from time to time to delete files using the **ERASE** command.

To erase the database file **SALESREP.DBF** from a disk located in the **A** drive, the appropriate form of the **ERASE** command would be

ERASE A:SALESREP.DBF

To erase all backup versions of text files saved on a disk located in the **A** drive and created using Wordstar, all of which would have automatically been given the extension **.BAK**, the appropriate **ERASE** command would be

ERASE A:*.BAK

To erase all files on a disk in the **A** drive, the appropriate **ERASE** command would be

ERASE A:*.*

Because such a command will erase all files which, in normal circumstances cannot be resurrected, most versions of DOS would greet this command with the question

Are you sure (Y/N) ?

response to which has to be confirmed by both the **Y** key (for YES) and the **ENTER** key.

Renaming files

(use of the **RENAME** command)

In most packages, before a backup file with the **.BAK** filename extension could be used, it would have to be given the correct filename extension required by the package. Such a procedure would be necessary if the most recent version of the file had accidentally been erased and the user wished to use the backup file as a substitute. The renaming of a backup file with a **.BAK** extension on a disk in the **A** drive to a text file with an extension **.TXT**, could be achieved using the **RENAME** command as follows

RENAME A:BCPCHAP2.BAK A:BCPCHAP2.TXT

Typing file contents to screen

(use of the **TYPE** command)

Any file containing text can be shown on the screen using the **TYPE** command. When invoked the text will scroll rapidly down the screen but can be halted by using **^S** (i.e. the **Ctrl** key used in conjunction with the **S** character key or alternatively, where it is provided on the keyboard, the **PAUSE** key). Many software applications packages issue latest changes/modifications in a file named **README.TXT** or **READ.ME** which can be read on screen by using the **TYPE** command

TYPE README.TXT

Printing files on a printer

(use of the **PRINT** command)

Any text file can be printed on a printer attached to the microcomputer (as long as it has paper in it and is switched on!) with the **PRINT** command. For example

    PRINT README.TXT

will produce a paper copy of the file mentioned in the previous sub-section. The file will be printed using the printer's default settings. These settings can be changed (e.g. to give a different size of print) but this is beyond the scope of this book.

A1.3 External DOS commands

External DOS commands are similar in operation to internal commands but are available from additional DOS files other than the standard **COMMAND.COM** file. Hence, for external commands to operate, the specific DOS file for that command (which will have the same name as the command) must be available on disk.

Disk copying

(use of the **DISKCOPY** command for which the file **DISKCOPY.COM** must be available on disk)

Particularly for producing a backup disk which is identical to the user's working disk, the **DISKCOPY** command not only copies all files across but also formats the target disk automatically if required. To produce an identical copy of a disk given that, as with most PCs today only a single floppy disk drive is provided, the DOS command

    DISKCOPY A: A:

could be invoked. This would instruct the user to load the source disk (i.e. the disk being copied) in the **A** drive initially and subsequently to remove this disk and replace it with the target disk (i.e. the disk being copied to). If the target disk had not already been formatted, this procedure would happen automatically. For most disk-copying the source and target disks need to be inserted into and removed from the disk drive twice.

Formatting a disk

(use of the **FORMAT** command for which the **FORMAT.COM** file must be available on disk)

Before any floppy disk can be used for storing information it must have been previously formatted. The formatting process magnetically marks the surface of the disk into tracks and sectors and also creates a disk directory. The formatting process is usually used with new disks but can obviously be used with disks which have been previously used if none of the files on that disk are still required.

To format a disk in the **A** drive and to give it a volume name (i.e. give the disk a name that will be displayed by the **DIR**ectory command) the required simplest **FORMAT** command could be

FORMAT A:/V

However, the **FORMAT** command now varies considerably depending on the machine in use, the version of DOS, the capacity of the disk drive being used and the proposed capacity of the disk being formatted — users should ask for advice from their local expert on the exact form of the command for their situation.

A1.4 Hard disk commands

Because a hard disk is capable of containing many thousands of files, it is necessary to divide up the available storage space on a hard disk into a series of tree-structured directories and sub-directories within which files can be stored, each sub-directory being conceptually similar to an individual floppy disk.

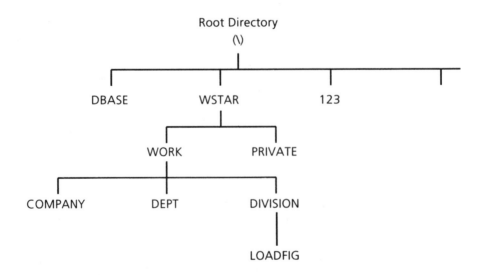

Figure 35 A typical DOS directory structure

The design and structure of directories and sub-directories on a hard disk is created by each individual user and typically would extend to two or three levels below the root directory — the first directory of the hard disk that the user will initially be located in. A typical hard-disk directory structure for a personal computer user is shown in Figure 35.

The thinking behind this particular structure of directories is that the user requires to divide word-processing (**WSTAR**) files broadly between those relating to **WORK** and **PRIVATE** correspondence and within **WORK** correspondence subdivide files into those relating to the company (**COMPANY**), the department (**DEPT**) or division (**DIVISION**). For illustrative purposes, within the sub-directory **DIVISION** a file **LOADFIG** has been saved.

Changing a directory

(using the **CD** command)

The **CD** (change directory) command allows the user to specify which of the many directories or sub-directories is to be the active (or default) directory. With regard to the situation depicted in Figure 35, to change from the root (\) or indeed any other directory to the **WSTAR** directory, the required **CD** command would be

   CD\WSTAR

where the inclusion of the backslash character (\) ensures that the **WSTAR** directory is sought from the root directory not the current directory, which might be different.

Given that the user were already located in the **WSTAR** directory, to change from the **WSTAR** directory to the **DIVISION** sub-directory, the required **CD** command would be

   CD DIVISION

although clearly the command

   CD\WSTAR\DIVISION

would be more comprehensive and would locate the user in the correct sub-directory irrespective of the current directory.

To return to the root directory the command would be

   CD\

and to move up the directory tree from say the **DIVISION** sub-directory to the **WSTAR** directory (i.e. back one directory) would require the command

   CD..

[NOTE: In using hard disks, it helps to use a convention that states that a sub-directory becomes a directory in its own right when it is made active using the **CD** command. Hence in the structure shown in Figure 35 the command **CD WSTAR** makes **WSTAR** the active directory containing the two sub-directories **WORK** and **DIVISION**]

Making a directory

(using the **MD** command)

The **MD** (make directory) command is used to create new directories or sub-directories. The simplest way of using the **MD** command is to create sub-directories relative to the active directory, i.e. that one to which the user has most recently changed.

Hence, in the tree-structured directory shown in Figure 35, the **COMPANY** sub-directory could have been created from the **WORK** directory using the command

   MD COMPANY

Removing a directory

(using the **RD** command)

The **RD** (remove directory) command is used to remove (i.e. erase) a previously created sub-directory. Before it can be used the user must ensure that all files located in that sub-directory have themselves been erased using an appropriate **ERASE** command. Thus in the tree-structured directory shown in Figure 35, if all the files in the **DEPT** directory had been erased and the user was located in the **WORK** directory as the active directory, the command

   RD DEPT

would remove the **DEPT** directory.

Creating a directory path

(using the **PATH** command)

It is often not convenient to organize that all the files required of a particular application be located in the same active directory. To allow the computer's operating system to locate files which may be held elsewhere than the active directory specified for the application, it is possible at the outset to create a **PATH** command which indicates alternative directories in which files required by the application may be located other than that originally specified. **PATH** commands are most usefully contained in an **AUTOEXEC.BAT** file, but for the situation depicted would be of the form

PATH = C:\;\LOTUS;\DBASE;\HARVARD;\WSTAR;\WSTAR\WORK; etc.

A1.5 Special DOS facilities

The GRAPHICS.COM file

The **GRAPHICS.COM** file is a special DOS file which when loaded allows the user to screen-dump graphics. Screen-dumping is a DOS facility which simply dumps (i.e. reproduces) whatever currently appears on the screen to a printer.

To dump the contents of the screen to a printer the **Shift** and **PrintScrn** keys must be used simultaneously. Textual information will always be dumped but graphics only if the **GRAPHICS.COM** file has been loaded with the **GRAPHICS** command. This loading is normally done at the start of a computing session using the **AUTOEXEC.BAT** file as is illustrated in the following section.

The AUTOEXEC.BAT file

As has been indicated earlier, when a DOS-based PC or equivalent is switched on the computer immediately looks for the disk files containing the DOS operating system before it can function.

Equally, when the operating system files are successfully loaded, DOS in turn looks for a file named **AUTOEXEC.BAT.** and automatically executes the commands held within that file. This facility can save the user a tremendous amount of time when starting a computing session since several commands required to initialize the system, which would otherwise have to be keyed in on each occasion, can automatically be executed without any user input. Today the contents of the **AUTOEXEC.BAT** file can be rather complex and are usually created by those installing the machine.

The F3 function key

A little known but very useful DOS facility is that the function key **F3** repeats the same DOS command as previously entered by the user. This command is then executed by pressing the ENTER key. Thus, when searching through a series of floppy disks to find a file for example, having specified a DIR command such as

DIR A:/W

this command can be repeated after each disk change simply by pressing the **F3** function key. Alternatively the latest command can be edited when recalled by the **F3** function key if a slightly different DOS command is to be created. Also useful in this connection is that repeated use of the right-hand arrow (➡) key will reproduce a previous DOS command one character at a time.

The warm boot

Occasionally a computer crashes or locks-out for some reason; rather than switching the computer off and then on again (a cold boot) the user can achieve a similar effect by pressing the **Ctrl**, **Alt** and **Del** keys simultaneously. This warm boot procedure resets the computer, reloads DOS and also executes the commands in an **AUTOEXEC.BAT** file if this is available. Note that since the Windows operating system 'sits on top of' DOS, and insists that users exit Windows in an orderly fashion so that files can be closed properly, a warm boot is not usually allowed in a Windows environment.

The foregoing description has been an attempt to describe operating systems in general and the facilities offered by the PC/MS-DOS operating system in particular. The facilities described are those considered the most essential to the average user but in no way cover all those available.

Appendix 2
Spreadsheets (2):
macros and menus

Modes of operation of spreadsheet packages

The vast majority of spreadsheet applications are carried out by end-users who enter figures and operate the menu-driven command structure manually. This ignores the programming potential which underpins all spreadsheet packages and which allows for the use of a spreadsheet package as the *engine* for developing bespoke menu-driven systems. Such systems allow professional systems developers (and even enthusiastic amateurs!) with a knowledge of the spreadsheet package's programming language, to create systems which can then be operated in a bespoke, menu-driven environment by users who require no knowledge of spreadsheets and their command structure.

The simplest version of a spreadsheet program (or *macro*) is the *one-key* macro, the creation of which is now described.

One-key macros within a spreadsheet

The Lotus commands which would be required of a user using Lotus 1-2-3 in a manual mode to re-save an existing spreadsheet file and print out a specified range of the spreadsheet would be as shown in the table on page 194.

The 20 key strokes indicated in the table can be reproduced by a single keystroke combination, say **AltS** (the Alt and S keys used in combination) by creating a one-key macro as follows.

Initially, locate the cursor well away from the main data section of the spreadsheet in a location that will not be used for anything else, say A100. Then at A100 enter the text:

'/fs~r/pparA1.G30~gpq

where the opening (') single quote or apostrophe character ensures that the following keystrokes are accepted as text and not actual commands, and the (~) tilde character is used to represent the equivalent of the RETURN key.

Subsequently create the cell A100 as a named range with the special range name \S.

When this operation is complete, the 20 keystrokes required to save the new file and print out the latest version of the spreadsheet will be invoked simply by holding down the **Alt** key in conjunction with the **S** character key.

Number	Keystroke	Function
1	/	Activates command menu
2	f	File command
3	s	Save command (current filename will be offered as first choice)
4	[RETURN]	Accepts first choice offer
5	r	Replace option
6	/	Activates command menu
7	p	Print command
8	p	Printer option
9	a	Align printer option
10	r	Range option
11	A	
12	1	
13	.	Defines print
14	G	range A1.G30
15	3	
16	0	
17	[RETURN]	
18	g	Go option
19	p	Page feed option
20	q	Quit option

Menu-driven systems within a spreadsheet

As early as 1983, Release 1a of Lotus 1-2-3 contained not only over fifty @functions for mathematical, financial, date, logical, trigonometric and other applications but also eight so-called /x macro commands which provided programming facilities for:

- Menu creation with up to eight options selected either by cursor positioning or unique first character

- Unconditional program jumps

- Conditional program jumps

- Subroutine branching and return

- Requests for the manual input of text

- Requests for manual input of numeric data

In 1986, with Release 2.01 of Lotus 1-2-3, some forty further programming commands (or macrowords) were provided offering a complete programming environment while still retaining the basic spreadsheet facilities that have maintained the popularity of the spreadsheet concept, namely:

- The naming of a variable based on its position within a two-dimensional matrix

- Simple formulae which can be copied

- Graphical facilities with the capability of specifying up to six variables within line and x-y graphs, bar, stacked bar and pie charts together with automatic or manual setting of axis scales

- Numerous @functions such as @SUM( ), @AVG( ), etc.

- Alphabetic and numeric sorting facilities

- Special facilities; such as regression and matrix inversion

Competitor spreadsheets such as Supercalc5 and Excel and, in the shareware market, AsEasy, also offer similar programming infrastructures; thus ensuring that menu-driven systems involving the manipulation of numerical data can be developed using the majority of modern spreadsheet packages. This parallels the development of menu-driven systems for the manipulation of database information using command-driven, flexible database packages such as Borland's dBASE. Figure 36 illustrates successive screens from a menu-driven forecasting package Lotus-FORMAN[1] from which it can be seen that each successive screen is introduced as an option to the preceding screen and that such options are chosen from menus which are designed by the developer and

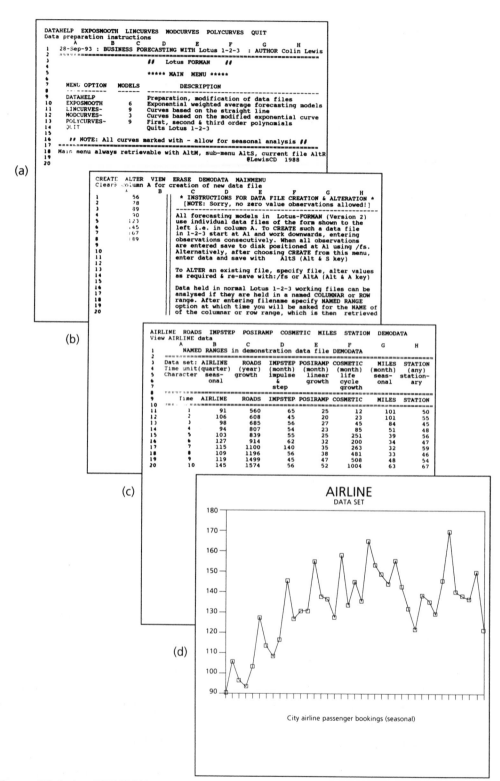

Figure 36 Lotus FORMAN screens

are not standard Lotus menus.

Figure 36 demonstrates the use of this procedure by illustrating a sequence of four screens taking from the forecasting package Lotus-FORMAN developed by one of the authors[1]. Inspection of the menu's associated screens should convince readers that the menus designed for the operation of a forecasting package are not standard Lotus 1-2-3 menus and that each successive screen is a menu option of the previous screen. Hence, screen (b) results from choosing menu option DATAHELP from screen (a), screen (c) results from the menu option DEMODATA from screen (b), and screen (d) results from menu option AIRLINE from screen (c).

Conclusion

Spreadsheets are one of the most popular software packages developed for microcomputers. Such packages offer a variety of facilities mainly associated with manipulating numeric data but also do offer limited database facilities.

Although the majority of applications of spreadsheets function in a manual mode, most spreadsheets do possess a programming structure which can be used to develop bespoke menu-driven systems.

Reference
1. Lewis, C.D. *Business Forecasting in a Lotus 1-2-3 Environment*, Wiley, 1989.

Appendix 3
Database packages: further facilities

Indexing records

One of the most powerful facilities of any flexible database package is the ability to sort or index records such that they can be displayed as if arranged in any specified order or sequence. Thus, virtually instantaneously, records can be presented, for example, in:

- Alphabetical order of surname

- Descending order of annual turnover

- Ascending or descending order of age.

From a technical point of view, sorting is a process which takes information from one database, sorts that information and produces a second database of equal size to the original. This obviously is a very wasteful process (in terms of the amount of disk space required) to store what is, essentially, the same information in two different forms. Because sorting procedures are so clearly inefficient in terms of disk utilization, most database packages also offer users an indexing procedure for viewing records in a number of pre-specified orders or sequences.

The indexing process within a database package is based on the fact that each and every record within a database is uniquely identified by its record number. Thus, if an index file can be arranged in such a way that:

- Just the unique record numbers are held in the desired order with accompanying relevant fields

- The database can be viewed through the numbering sequence of records held in the index file

then the records in a database could be viewed in any required order.

Because an index file contains only record numbers and the contents of the field or fields making up the index *key,* an indexing process requires very little additional disk storage space. In general, index files will therefore be significantly smaller than the database file from which they are derived. Typically a 500 Kbyte database could be viewed with an index file of only 2

Kbytes, whereas a 500 Kbyte database when sorted produces an additional 500 Kbyte database.

Since index files are relatively small (in terms of the disk space they occupy) and the indexing process is technically very efficient, many database packages allow up to seven index files to be linked simultaneously to a single database. In such situations records will be viewed in the order of the first named index file, but all other index files will be immediately updated should records within the database be deleted, appended or modified.

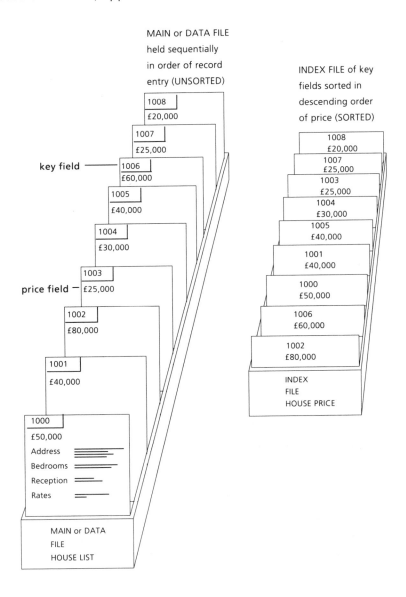

Figure 37 Physical analogy of a database file

To further illustrate the mechanics of the indexing process, a physical analogy of a database file and its associated index file is shown in Figure 37. In this illustrative example the database file consists of information relating to houses for sale and the index file is constructed on a *key* based on a single numeric field, namely house price, thus allowing the records to be viewed in ascending or descending order of price. Because only record numbers and house prices are held in this index file, it is apparent that it must occupy much less space than its associated database file.

Indexing on a character field can present records in alphabetical or reverse alphabetical order. Indexing on a numeric field can present records in ascending or descending order.

Figures 38 and 39 show the order of presentation of records in a database when indexing on a key containing just a single field. In these two examples the listings of records from the **STAFF** database (shown originally as Figure 13) are shown in *alphabetical* order of name and *ascending* order of salary respectively.

Database: STAFF				Page 1
#	COMPANY	DIV	DEPT	NAME	SALARY
6	UK MICRO	EXPORT	PROD	ABRAHAMS B R	21450
3	UK MICRO	EXPORT	R & D	BRYANT P	24000
14	EURO MICRO	HOME	R & D	BUNNAG A	28500
10	EURO MICRO	HOME	PROD	EDWARDS J	25600
13	UK MICRO	EXPORT	PROD	GAGARIN Y	19000
11	EURO MICRO	HOME	PROD	GRANT B	22500
1	UK MICRO	HOME	MKTG	JONES W	27000
9	UK MICRO	EXPORT	MKTG	LEWIS C	27000
5	EURO MICRO	EXPORT	MKTG	LITTLE J	25250
12	EURO MICRO	EXPORT	MKTG	LOESER G	19180
7	UK MICRO	HOME	MKTG	PARMAR B	24750
8	EURO MICRO	EXPORT	R & D	SHIRES S	26100
15	EURO MICRO	HOME	R & D	SOHAL D S	22000
2	EURO MICRO	EXPORT	PROD	THOMAS P J	24750
4	EURO MICRO	HOME	PROD	YOUNGER W	18000

Figure 38 Database records listed in alphabetical order of name

#	COMPANY	DIV	DEPT	NAME	SALARY
4	EURO MICRO	HOME	PROD	YOUNGER W	18000
13	UK MICRO	EXPORT	PROD	GAGARIN Y	19000
12	EURO MICRO	EXPORT	MKTG	LOESER G	19180
6	UK MICRO	EXPORT	PROD	ABRAHAMS B R	21450
15	EURO MICRO	HOME	R & D	SOHAL D S	22000
11	EURO MICRO	HOME	PROD	GRANT B	22500
3	UK MICRO	EXPORT	R & D	BRYANT P	24000
2	EURO MICRO	EXPORT	PROD	THOMAS P J	24750
7	UK MICRO	HOME	MKTG	PARMAR B	24750
5	EURO MICRO	EXPORT	MKTG	LITTLE J	25250
10	EURO MICRO	HOME	PROD	EDWARDS J	25600
8	EURO MICRO	EXPORT	R & D	SHIRES S	26100
1	UK MICRO	HOME	MKTG	JONES W	27000
9	UK MICRO	EXPORT	MKTG	LEWIS C	27000
14	EURO MICRO	HOME	R & D	BUNNAG A	28500

Figure 39 Database records listed in ascending order of salary

Note that record numbers are no longer in numerical order, as was the case in Figure 13 when the database was unindexed.

The key on which an index file is created can be any single field within the record structure, as already discussed, or a combination of several fields. To illustrate this facility, Figure 40 shows records presented using an index file based on a *key* comprised of a combination of four character fields namely **COMPANY**, **DIVISION**, **DEPT** (department) and **NAME** (surname). Readers should note from this listing that records are arranged:

● Initially alphabetically by **COMPANY**

● Subsequently within **COMPANY** alphabetically by **DIVISION**

● Subsequently within **DIVISION** by **DEPT**

● Finally within **DEPT** alphabetically by **NAME**.

```
Database: STAFF                                                    Page 1

  #    COMPANY        DIV        DEPT     NAME            SALARY

  5    EURO MICRO     EXPORT     MKTG     LITTLE J         25250

 12    EURO MICRO     EXPORT     MKTG     LOESER G         19180

  2    EURO MICRO     EXPORT     PROD     THOMAS P J       24750

  8    EURO MICRO     EXPORT     R & D    SHIRES S         26100

 10    EURO MICRO     HOME       PROD     EDWARDS J        25600

 11    EURO MICRO     HOME       PROD     GRANT B          22500

  4    EURO MICRO     HOME       PROD     YOUNGER W        18000

 14    EURO MICRO     HOME       R & D    BUNNAG A         28500

 15    EURO MICRO     HOME       R & D    SOHAL D S        22000

  9    UK MICRO       EXPORT     MKTG     LEWIS C          27000

  6    UK MICRO       EXPORT     PROD     ABRAHAMS B R     21450

 13    UK MICRO       EXPORT     PROD     GAGARIN Y        19000

  3    UK MICRO       EXPORT     R & D    BRYANT P         24000

  1    UK MICRO       HOME       MKTG     JONES W          27000

  7    UK MICRO       HOME       MKTG     PARMAR B         24750
```

Figure 40 Database records listed in an order based on multiple keys

Indexing is a powerful feature of flexible database packages. By allowing the
user to present records in any desired order or sequence, records with common
field contents can be collected together in groups for the production of
financial information in the form of totals, sub-totals and sub-sub-totals within
a reporting facility.

For searching purposes indexing is also important since, if records are held un-
indexed, a search for records meeting a specified search criterion will have to
start at the first record and continue through every record in the database. With
a database indexed on the field which constitutes the search *key*, the searching
procedure can go straight to the relevant set of records which match the *key*. A
dictionary is a good example of a database indexed to facilitate searching.

Reporting from a database

Most interactions with database packages, be those packages menu driven or command driven, are in the form of *exception reports.* Such exception reports bring to the attention of the user details of records held in the database which meet certain specified criteria and do so in the form of printed reports with features such as:

- Automatic page numbering

- Automatic system date insertion

- Printing of fixed or temporary headings on successive pages

- Column headings repeated on successive pages

- Optional sub-totalling facilities for numeric fields with sub-totals being triggered by the changing of the contents of a specified character field. For this feature to operate correctly records must be indexed.

- If required, sub-totals can be used to produce a page feed so that individual pages can be separated for distribution to those responsible for the group, division, company, etc. to whom the sub-total relates.

Most flexible database packages offer a *report generator* which can be used to create report form files which specify the details required by the package to produce reports with a pre-specified layout. Obviously the actual physical reports produced by a single report form file will vary in content as time progresses, since the population of records held within the database will vary from the issuing of one report to the next depending on the number of records being erased, appended and altered (for example, a list of current outstanding invoices). In addition, reports produced by the same report form file will vary, since the criteria that control which records are included in a report are independent of the report form file with which they are used.

Reports produced from a database can either be detailed or summary in form.

Detailed reports

Detailed reports include details of field contents, as specified by the user, for all records which meet the selection criterion for inclusion in the report. Examining the features of the detailed report shown as Figure 41, which is again derived from the personnel database originally shown as Figure 13, readers should note:

- Only records that meet the criterion that **SALARY>20000** are presented to the report form file

- Records are presented to the report form file indexed in alphabetical order of **NAME** within **COMPANY** order. This ensures that sub-totals are triggered in the correct position, namely when the contents of the **COMPANY** field change.

- The heading:

  STAFF WITH SALARIES OVER £20000

  is a temporary heading used only for this particular printed report

- The heading:

  PERSONNEL CURRENTLY EMPLOYED

  ===============================

  BY EURO MICRO & UK MICRO

  ==========================

  is a permanent heading saved within the structure of the report form file which will appear on all reports and, therefore, needs to be rather bland to accommodate any report that might be generated

- Column headings line up with appropriate field contents

- The contents of the **COMPANY** field are not generally included as the contents of a column but are displayed at the start of each new sub-total block, i.e.

  ** COMPANY: EURO MICRO

- Sub-totals are printed at the end of each sub-total block as triggered by the **COMPANY** field's contents changing as indexed records are presented alphabetically in company order

- A grand (or overall) total is printed at the end of the report

- Page numbers and date of printing (in this case in the American format of mm/dd/yy) are inserted automatically.

Summary reports

Summary reports do not include the detail of field contents for individual records included within the report but only display sub-totals (or indeed sub-sub-totals) of numeric fields. Such a summary report could, for example, be used by the manager of a company requiring to know the salary bill of constituent companies within a group of companies or departments within a single company but who was not interested in the salary details of individual employees within those companies or departments.

```
STAFF WITH SALARIES OVER £20000          Page 1


PERSONNEL CURRENTLY EMPLOYED              08/30/93

============================
BY EURO MICRO AND UK MICRO

========================


DIVISION     DEPARTMENT     NAME          SALARY


** COMPANY: EURO MICRO
HOME         R & D          BUNNAG A      28500
HOME         PROD           EDWARDS J     25600
HOME         PROD           GRANT B       22500
EXPORT       MKTG           LITTLE J      25250
EXPORT       R & D          SHIRES S      26100
HOME         R & D          SOHAL D S     22000
EXPORT       PROD           THOMAS P J    24750
** SUB-TOTAL **                           174700


** COMPANY: UK MICRO
EXPORT       PROD           ABRAHAMS B R  21450
EXPORT       R & D          BRYANT P      24000
HOME         MKTG           JONES W       27000
EXPORT       MKTG           LEWIS C       27000
HOME         MKTG           PARMAR B      24750
** SUB-TOTAL **                           124200


*** TOTAL ***                             298900
```

Figure 41 A detailed report from a personnel database

Examining the features of the summary report shown as Figure 42, which is again derived from the personnel database originally shown as Figure 13, readers should note:

- In this case all records in the database are presented to the report form file

- Although not apparent from the printed report, records must have been presented to the report form file indexed in **COMPANY** order. This ensures that sub-totals are triggered in the correct position, namely when the contents of the **COMPANY** field change.

- The heading:

  SALARY SUMMARY: ALL EMPLOYEES

  is a temporary heading used only for this particular printed report

- The heading:

  PERSONNEL CURRENTLY EMPLOYED

  ==============================

  BY EURO MICRO & UK MICRO

  =========================

  is a permanent heading saved within the structure of the report form file which will appear on all reports and, therefore, needs to be rather bland to accommodate any report that might be generated

- Column headings and details of field contents are only included for **NUMERIC** fields for which sub-totals or sub-sub-totals have been specified

- The contents of the **COMPANY** field are displayed at the start of each new sub-total block, i.e.

  ** COMPANY: EURO MICRO

- Sub-totals are printed at the end of each sub-total block as triggered by the **COMPANY** field's contents changing

- A grand (or overall) total is printed at the end of the report

- Page numbers and date of printing (in this case in the American format of mm/dd/yy) are inserted automatically.

```
SALARY SUMMARY: ALL EMPLOYEES          Page 1


PERSONNEL CURRENTLY EMPLOYED           08/30/93

============================
BY EURO MICRO AND UK MICRO

========================


SALARY OF EMPLOYEES

=================


** COMPANY: EURO MICRO
** SUBTOTAL **          211880


** COMPANY: UK MICRO
** SUBTOTAL **          143200


*** TOTAL ***           355080
```

Figure 42 A summary report from a personnel database

Relational databases

The best of current flexible database packages go beyond indexed files to
provide some of the facilities of so-called relational database packages. These
are particularly useful where different database applications use some of the
same data; for example, a stock file and a market share file might use the same
list of product names. One of the main goals of relational database systems is to
avoid the duplication of data. We have already mentioned this in the context of
sorting (as opposed to indexing) records within a database, but this applies just
as much to the contents of the records. If one file (the customer file, say)
contains customer names and their associated customer addresses, then having
both customer names and customer addresses in another file (the invoice file,
say) is an unnecessary duplication of data. Duplication is not only a waste of
storage space but, more importantly, creates a problem in maintaining the
integrity of the data whenever the database is updated. In particular, a new
application which requires the sharing of previously exclusive data involves
considerable programming effort in order to set up the new database files
without compromising the functioning of the existing application.

The relational approach is to enable all data to be shared by all applications. Thus, rather than say an invoicing application and a stock control application each containing its own data on product descriptions, the product codes and descriptions would be held in a separate file (a data table) and accessed by both applications to retrieve the descriptions as necessary. With this *data-oriented* approach, as opposed to the older *application-oriented* one, the data files are organized according to the nature of the information in them, and thus are not affected by the introduction of new applications. A new application simply involves adding any new data tables necessary to the system.

Despite these advantages, relational database packages are not a panacea for all problems of database system development. A fair description might be that they are an answer to most of the structural problems which a database designer or administrator faces. This does not take account, however, of system performance issues, especially speed. This is an area where the basic philosophy of the relational database approach actually causes problems, because the data required by any particular application will not have been customized for it. Thus, roughly speaking, the more tables which must be accessed by an application, the slower it will run. Hence the designers' concerns over structural problems have been replaced with concerns about performance problems, and this is where much of the expertise in relational database design lies. Applications requiring access to many tables may generate many read/write head movements across the magnetic disks used to store the information, which can result in an unacceptably long response time to retrieve the information (in practice, 3 seconds or more could be considered unacceptable), as well as an increase in the likelihood of breakdown of the physical disk drive units. The different relational database packages have various techniques which may be used to improve response time and reduce input/output costs. When refining the design of a new relational database, the system designer will apply the appropriate techniques, bearing in mind the expected importance of the applications to be included. As computer systems are dynamic, other problems will occur once the system has been in use and so the database administrator (DBA) will also have to use the techniques available in the particular package to *tune* the relational database system.

Index